STARTING FROM ZERO.
RECONSTRUCTING
DOWNTOWN NEW YORK
MICHAEL SORKIN

START FROM

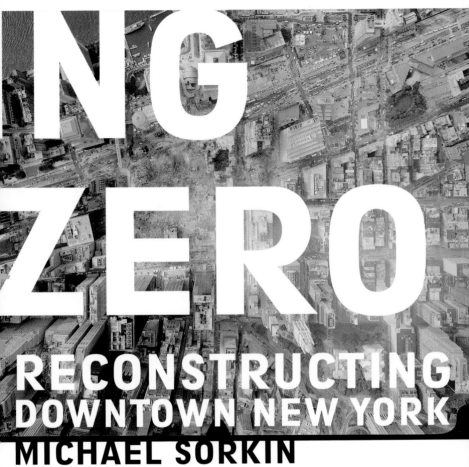

NG
ZERO

RECONSTRUCTING
DOWNTOWN NEW YORK

MICHAEL SORKIN

ROUTLEDGE
TAYLOR & FRANCIS GROUP

FOR THE VICTIMS

PUBLISHED IN 2003
BY ROUTLEDGE
29 WEST 35TH STREET
NEW YORK, NY 10001
WWW.ROUTLEDGE-NY.COM

PUBLISHED IN GREAT BRITAIN
BY ROUTLEDGE
11 NEW FETTER LANE
LONDON EC4P 4EE
WWW.ROUTLEDGE.CO.UK

ROUTLEDGE IS AN IMPRINT OF THE TAYLOR AND FRANCIS GROUP.

PRINTED AND BOUND IN HONG KONG THROUGH ASIA PACIFIC OFFSET, INC.

10 9 8 7 6 5 4 3 2 1

LIBRARY OF CONGRESS CATALOGING-IN-PUBLICATION DATA

SORKIN, MICHAEL, 1948—
    STARTING FROM ZERO : RECONSTRUCTING DOWNTOWN NEW YORK / MICHAEL SORKIN.
        P. CM.
    ISBN 0-415-94734-0 (HARDCOVER : ALK. PAPER) — ISBN 0-415-94737-5
(PBK. : ALK. PAPER)
    1. ARCHITECTURE—NEW YORK (STATE)—NEW YORK—21ST CENTURY—DESIGNS AND PLANS. 2.
NEW YORK (N.Y.)—BUILDINGS, STRUCTURES, ETC. 3. MANHATTAN
(NEW YORK, N.Y.)—BUILDINGS, STRUCTURES, ETC. 4. CITY PLANNING—NEW YORK (STATE)—
NEW YORK—HISTORY—21ST CENTURY. 5. WORLD TRADE CENTER
(NEW YORK, N.Y.) I. TITLE.
    NA735.N5S67 2003
    711'.4'097471—DC21

                                                                        2003008977

CONTENTS

INTRODUCTION

ON THE MORNING OF THE 11TH I SLEPT A LITTLE LATER THAN USUAL AND, FOR SOME REASON, DID NOT TURN ON THE TELEVISION WHEN I WOKE UP, LYING FOR A TIME IN A PRE-COFFEE HAZE. It was election day and I eventually pulled myself together to head downstairs to vote on the way to work. Leaving my building, I turned right towards Sixth Avenue and immediately noticed something was amiss: traffic did not seem to be flowing and the street was filled with people looking south. My immediate assumption was an accident, a police action. Getting to the corner, I turned my gaze downtown and—thinking that what had happened was in the street—did not immediately see the object of the crowd's attention. And then I looked up.

The north tower of the World Trade Center was gashed and flames were licking at its façade well up. Next to it—where the south tower should have stood—was a shroud of gray smoke. People with radios gave me the news: planes had smashed into the tower, another had struck the Pentagon. What I saw from a mile uptown did not seem severe; fire, yes, but surely one that could be controlled. So improbable, so out of the range of my thinking, was the idea that the towers could actually fall, I dismissed what other onlookers were telling me, that the column of smoke I was staring at concealed a void, that one of the towers had already collapsed. Reassured from the depths of my architect's expertise, I simply assumed that it was impossible. Within minutes the second tower was also gone.

Rushing back home, I tried frantically to contact people. My wife was stranded at LaGuardia. My parents—who live a few miles from the Pentagon—were safe. What next? The TV was on by now and the repeated reports became numbing. I decided to go vote, thinking this was democracy's riposte to terror. On the way to the school that serves as our polling place, I met my friend George, hurrying to retrieve his daughter from a school further downtown. The street was filled with the rush of anxiety as people ran to find kids, friends, spouses. The polls were already closed, the election cancelled, and the sidewalk out front was filled with parents and kids. Heading down the block to St. Vincent's hospital to donate blood, I found a queue snaking around the block, hundreds of people, a matter of hours to wait on line. And so I began walking down towards my studio, ten blocks north of the Trade Center.

Emergency vehicles screamed down streets now clear of traffic. From downtown, a numb crowd moved north in silent but measured flight. As I made my way south more and more people were covered in white ash. Below Canal Street, ash was falling and papers swirled and fell from the sky. The column of smoke rose and rose and everywhere was a horrific and unmistakable smell. Police barricades were appearing and I was just able to reach my building. The phones were out and I sat at the window staring at the maelstrom and listening to the radio. Eventually, the building was evacuated for fear of gas explosions and I trudged back north to reconsider everything.

This book is a record of a year and half of responses to the horrendous tragedy of September 11. It is, in many ways, very narrow in its focus, about the role of architecture and planning in an irrevocably altered New York. The discourse of reconstruction arose quickly and assumed a wide variety of guises and roles, eventually dominating all discussion of the event. Almost immediately there was a division between two reflexive responses: to rebuild intensively as both symbol and substance of regeneration and as rejoinder to the terror and, on the other hand, to leave the site free of commercial building, a permanent memorial. This work is both a reflection of the victory of the first approach and a record of alternative ideas.

The site's importance in the commemoration of the lives lost assumed peculiar character given the horror of the incineration and the resulting fragmentary remains of so many victims. As the task of recovery bore on, it became clear that this was a gravesite without graves, without bodies. The form of embodiment that symbols would thus be obliged to take was a terrible one, like a commemoration at Hiroshima or Auschwitz. This was not Gettysburg, not a place for serried tombstones; not a military site, however much the terror was described as an act of war. The massacre was of civilians, and they had been reduced to dust. We had all breathed their flesh.

My own feelings about the nature of commemoration began to take some shape after an early visit to the devastated site, seeing it up close for the first time in all its twisted enormity, still burning, still dangerous. It was clear that few intact bodies were going to be found, and the city had announced that it was obtaining a large number of DNA kits, in order to help identify the torn remains. I was disturbed at this precision in the face of such enormity and wondered why this scrupulosity was necessary, thinking it would simply cause further dismay and distraction for the bereaved, obliged to find a strand of hair on a comb or donate cells to help match a member of the family.

Not long afterwards, I expressed this to a friend who brought me up short. He lived with someone who had spent many years involved with the families of the "disappeared" in Argentina, and she had reported that what was of greatest comfort to those whose children had been murdered and erased by the junta was some shred of certainty about their fate. Closure—that overworked word—came only with evidence that corroborated the finality known intuitively but unspeakable because the rituals of hope forbid it.

This insight suggested both the absolute importance of commemoration and the specificity with which it would invariably be understood. It also explained the infusion of the ground with the particulate of memory, some version of the sacred. Introduced at that moment was measurement—the process of recovery would involve repeated mapping of the meanings not just of the site but of the very idea of site. As the range of technical means were deployed to image and pin-point the fires still burning, the precise location of wreckage, the fallout of debris, the location of remains, a grim yet mesmerizing atlas was assembled that brought to public focus a way of seeing previously reserved for specialists and spies. Our gaze acquired a horrible but comforting objectivity.

This way of looking joined the mass media's saturation with imagery of the attack and its aftermath, helping to inscribe the place into a global repertoire of places of obsessive particularity, of celebrity. Marking and marking it again, Ground Zero grew in conceptual importance with every iteration of its visualization. And, precisely because the media chose to suppress any images of human forms, whether the desperate jumpers falling to their deaths or the tangled corpses retrieved from the wreckage, the agony was displaced onto the buildings. Like the crucifixion, the destruction proceeded through its stations: the strike, the fire, the rescue, the collapse, the grief. But the images were always of objects, or aircraft and buildings and rubble. Clearly, any resurrection would entail the rebirth of things, not of souls.

As if in compensation for this narrowed iconography of loss, the spontaneous memorials that grew in the aftermath of the event were terribly personal. The effusion of xerox copied images of victims that were posted by the thousands around town as distraught survivors sought to find their own disappeared was transformed into an archipelago of loss with the addition of flowers, candles, inscriptions, mementoes. In front of fire and police stations, near hospitals, around the site, in Union Square, images consolidated into poignant and excruciating memorials, profoundly apt to the nature of the tragedy. Not univalent cenotaphs or identical icons, they radiated what had become a horrific familiarity of difference. Bankers and busboys and brokers seen in wedding photos, graduation shots, and vacation snaps smiled out at us from the awful innocence of life.

Current efforts to produce a memorial pale beside the ephemeral perfection of this first collective expression of visualized grief. The titanic towers and sunken tumuli of the official offerings seem so trivial in their magnitude. Somehow, the need for an expression of grieving has become triumphalized as we wallow in the sanitized discourse of rebuilding better than ever. This year and a half has been all about the rigorous narrowing of expectations, the manufacture of a consensus that whatever formal solution be chosen for the site, its theme must be the rebirth — the resurrection — of the "life" that was there before, if not the very buildings. Indeed, according to some samplings of opinion, a majority of people would have preferred precisely that, the reconstruction of the towers as they were, perhaps a bit higher to symbolize resiliency and defiance.

It was hard not to have mixed feelings about the Trade Center. Their blankness and enormity were horrible and wonderful. Viewed from various distances — from Brooklyn, from New Jersey, from up-town, they were runic and remarkable. In their simple rectilinear profiles they were the perfect icons of the underlying symbolic meaning of the New York skyline, the long bar graph of value measuring the multiplied ground that is our great contribution to the physiognomy, economics, and art of the city.

Much of the towers' force came from their doubling. The willingness to construct in near adjacency two identical versions of the "tallest building in the world" surely spoke not simply to chest-thumping King-Kongism but to an idea of mass production. That they were clad in stainless steel and ornamented with the filigree of Sunbeam toasters carried them into the realm of consumer goods, sheer replicability, re-represented again in the 220 identical square floors within. The towers' artistic aspirations were derived from the excesses of "minimalism," from the notion that the larger and more simplified the work, the more minimal, and therefore the greater its content. As the largest minimalist objects on the planet, flaunting the idea of artistic singularity by their monumental duplication, the World Trade Center surely obtained some version of an almost totally deracinated sublime.

There were certainly pleasures associated with their size and with the precision of their construction. Standing on the observation deck, looking down on the Brooklyn Bridge — its heroic structure made Lilliputian — was to encounter the city in another way, like flying. Standing on the ground flush against the stainless column covers, looking skyward, was to learn the inner truth of perspective and something of the degree to which technology could conform precisely to a simple dream. They were simply awesome, so big they seemed to be cantilevered from the earth. That they inspired two great explorers—Philippe Petit and George Willig—should come as no surprise. Like early voyagers, each employed perilous but simple and precise instruments to take vertical and horizontal measurements of the forces at play, unknowingly foreshadowing disaster in their own risk.

As urbanism the towers were was just stupid but the fault was only partly theirs. True to themselves, they required the vapid podium on which they sat in order to deal with the slope of the site. To preserve their minimalist intensity they needed either level ground beneath them or the improbable act of leaning, beyond the technical and imaginative capabilities of the time. The result was the compressed mall space below grade, the labyrinthine distributor that joined subways, shops, elevators, bridges, escalators, parked cars, airport buses, and sorting crowds with grim efficiency. Instead of the city that had existed before, with its grid of streets and warren of small buildings, the whole was transferred underground, a city within the city, a little bit of Tokyo, trying for the Rockefeller Center concourse but without the design panache and absent the winning plaza above. The podium was dreadful, dividing north from south and—combined with the excessive width of West Street and the suburbanism of the World Financial Center and its vapid lawns—east from west.

9/11 produced an opportunity to think the site again and suddenly we were confronted by the awful paradox of this unfortunate fall. Loss always offers an opening, and the way we confront it goes to the heart of our ethical relationship to suffering and to the role of repair—of healing—in the process of moving on. As an architect, I wished to come to some terms with the character of this event by understanding something of the way in which its notional and physical spaces had been reinfused with meaning. As a citizen of the city, I wanted to engage with the collectivity in reinventing the possibility of the prospective in the wake of events that made the future impossible to simply take for granted.

This book is a meditation on disaster, my own way of coming to terms with it. To preserve the immediacy of these responses, they are presented largely as is and in a chronological sequence and I hope the reader will forgive any repetitiveness and a sometimes too pious tone.

The work represents a trajectory of feeling and opinion that covered quite a wide territory. Taken as a whole, they suggest a certain bitterness. Writing this at the beginning of March 2003, shortly after the "final" decision about a rebuilding strategy has been announced by the authorities, I cannot help feeling that the process has been corrupted by a meagerness of vision and a vanishing and over-aestheticized sense of loss. There is something nauseating about the celebratory atmosphere that has surrounded this act of "closure," about the haste of it all, and about the wheeling and dealing that lead up to it and continue as various parties vie for control of the site.

Most of all, the bitterness springs from a sense of a betrayal of the public's right of participation. I remain amazed at the number of editorials, articles, and public statements that celebrate the "openness"of the process of selecting this result and at the complicity of architects in reducing the content of the site to questions of design. The current conclusion has, in fact, been foregone for months. Indeed, it has been over a year since anyone seriously entertained any idea save the construction of millions of square feet of office space on the site, and the chosen scheme itself scarely departs conceptually from the schematic arrangements of last summer—the same *parti*, virtually the same arrangement of buildings, streets and open spaces, the same program. What has been added is a flaccid iconographic agenda and a grafted rhetoric of redemption and loss, so craven and self-serving as to make the skin creep.

What a waste of energy and imagination! The public outpouring in the months since 9/11 has been phenomenal, unlike anything the city has seen before. Never have so many been so absorbed in the forms and meanings of architecture and planning. Never have so many struggled to integrate ideas about what makes a city good and great with the physical techniques of achieving it. Never have so many understood the inequities of development. Never have so many so closely identified the forms of construction with the meaning of their own lives. The thousands of ideas simply glossed over, the failure to truly orchestrate a hearing for everyone with a cogent notion for the future of this place, is not simply a betrayal but the loss of an opportunity to cement a responsive, progressive, and instrumental relationship between the people and their servants in government, to make our future more collective rather than less.

Television these days is again crowded with images of buildings being destroyed from the air with incendiary hygiene and claims of high purpose. Our "smart" bombs kill no one, we are told; they just bust the bunkers and buildings of the evil doers. The military rationale sounds almost artistic: to produce shock and awe, urban and social renewal. Already, we are setting up the extra-govermental "authority" to rebuild the country we are triumphantly destroying and already, bids have gone out to giant, well-connected, corporations to do the job. It feels very familiar.

AFTER THE FALL

THIS TRAGEDY HAS A PARTICULAR BEARING FOR US AS ARCHITECTS: BUILDINGS CAUSED THE DEATHS OF THREE THOUSAND PEOPLE.
We are forced to examine fundamental assumptions, about the integrity of structure, about the logic of such concentrations of people, about height. What exactly is our responsibility here?

We are certainly shamed by our ambulance chasing colleagues who urge that we rebuild exactly as before. Or higher. Or more robust. Or four of them. The lease-holder has pledged to reconstruct imme-diately and has laid on a distinguished architect, ready to get back to business.

But something has shifted. We embarass ourselves by rushing out to spend again, by fantasizing about 150 story towers that will take an additional hour to evacuate when the next disaster strikes, by thinking about the next *thing*, by having no second thoughts about anything *we* might have done.

Visiting the site of the disaster in its immediate aftermath, I strug-gled to take in the somber beauty of twisted steel, the pulverized rubble that seemed too small to contain all of what was there before. I worried that something in me also had to die, some capacity for enjoyment, if only that shopworn sublime. At the grocery store an hour later, I cringed at choosing between a peach and a plum, at deciding among pleasures in a time of grief.

But the culture slogs on.

In a letter to the editor of the *Times*, Philipe de Monetebello calls the twisted remains a masterpiece.

Karlheinz Stockhuasuen declares the attack to be "the greatest work of art imaginable for the whole cosmos."

Broadway reopens with self-congratulatory bravado and unconscious irony. After the first post-disaster performance of *The Producers*, the cast takes the stage—dressed in their Nazi uniforms—to lead the audience in singing God Bless America.

Dan Rather weeps on Letterman.

In Kabul, our reporter visits a barbershop with a hidden camera. He has come to photograph an adolescent boy getting a "Titanic" haircut, like Leonardo DiCaprio's. Later, interviewing a turbaned Taliban, the correspondent reports what he has seen, rubbing the act of resistance in his bearded face. "Such things are not possible in Afghanistan," the mullah replies.

And for us? Clearly, some familiar way of facing the world must now die. The *Times* has already suggested post-modernity as a likely casualty. Certainly, this is not a moment for slippery relativism and ethical agnosticism, for the aestheticization of everything, for *any* obtrusive visuality. But how can we absorb the images presented to us day and night without simple recourse to old routines and strategies? How must we judge ourselves, judging?

The official demonization of the terrorists paints them as implacably other—pure evil—agents of nothing that we could have had any hand in producing. But the terrorists fascinate us, in part, because they are the dark side of something we have not simply predicted, but advanced. This extends beyond the intitial arming of and collaboration with Bin Laden during the Soviet Afghan war to deeper, more conceptual, connections. Al Quaeda—"the global network"—is just one tick away from our own global business as usual.

Osama bin Laden is one of us, the Patty Hearst of radical Islam, a trust fund revolutionary ready to go the extra mile. Scion of a family construction business with a client list to make the most jaded architect jealous, Bin Laden studied civil engineering and frequented the bars of Beirut, betraying an early penchant for structure and modernity, his own architecture.

Radicalized out of his gilded youth by the war in Afghanistan, Osama bin Laden became the extreme instance of globalization. His network of autonomous franchises regulated by infrequent signals from headquarters delivers its product with just-in-time precision, deploying the full spectrum of media — from cell phones to satellite links to complex and illicit private banking arrangements to high-tech forgeries — with incredible discipline and facility. The operatives who destroyed the Trade Center were well educated and able to quickly grasp the most sophisticated technology. These are not hopped up savages, dreaming of black-eyed virgins: these are our children.

Mohammed Atta, the apparent operational ringleader of the plot, was studying for a masters degree in city planning from a university in Hamburg which also housed the nucleus of a radical Islamic cell. His thesis advisor was quoted the other day speaking admiringly about Atta's diploma reaseach on the historic planning of Aleppo, Syria. The professor had not suspected the Atta was to be implicated in the most violent act of urbanism America had ever seen.

One of the most widely retailed images of the downfall of modernism is the implosion of The Pruitt Igoe towers in St. Louis, designed, like the Trade Center, by Minoru Yamasaki. This image has been absorbed into both architectural discourse and popular culture as a totem of corrective violence. Sept. 11 was the biggest implosion ever, staged in the most media saturated environment on the planet and captured from every angle, stamping out every other image. The unbelievable crash. The unbelievable collapse. The unbelievable aftermath. Too good not to broadcast, the media moguls have cleaned it up nicely for mass consumption and a PG rating by expunging shots of bodies falling, washing out the sight of blood, branding the event for easy, uncritical, consumption, to play over and over like Challenger or the Hindenberg or Kamikazes striking the carrier decks.

The global network that destroyed the towers was neural, enabled by the infrastructure of empire. Without the internet, no terror: these monsters are the dark side of the creature we have ourselves designed, operating in its unregulated space and driving its assumptions to their furthest conclusions. The killers visited a mad act of urban renewal on behalf of their own idea of one world. Down went not simply the leading architectural icon of global capital but the most concentrated symbol of human density, of the coming together that has, in one form or another, guided urbanism from its beginnings.

The most in-your-face image down here is on Canal Street, a billboard for the latest Schwarzenegger film with a huge Arnold in the foreground of the usual mayhem. The name of the film—the release of which has been delicately delayed by its producers—is "Collateral Damage." Perhaps it is time for us to address the collateral damage of our own enthusiasms. Perhaps it is time for architects (and Hollywood, and the fashion industry, and the news media and…) to curb their pandering to the culture of distress that is at the heart of, among other things, so-called "deconstructivism," to reconsider the infantile celebration of wounding, to stop *uncritically* indulging the soft pornographic fascination with the human or the architectural body rent and torn.

It is not too soon for us New Yorkers to question whether or not the forty or a hundred or a thousand billion dollars to be invested to make the city "whole" again belong on that small site downtown and not at every impoverished and suffering fringe of the city.

And might we begin to adjust our expectations and habits of consumption to really acknowledge and act upon the fact that a billion of us command and usurp the resources and livelihoods of the four billion whose misery we tolerate and extend with the blithe neo-liberalism of the global economy? Indeed, with the economy headquartered at the Trade Center?

Perhaps it is time for architects to cease their celebration of branding and "pure" communication to try to be of some real service to the planet.

Architectural theory has been talking for some years of building as the pure space of events.

Here is an event.

What now?

WHAT REMAINS

TRAFFIC RETURNED TO THE STREETS OF MY NEIGHBORHOOD TODAY AFTER THE CORDON WAS MOVED SOUTH TO CANAL STREET. It was the day of Bush's tardy visit and the sky was filled with the futile darting of fighter jets, commanding anxious looks upward with every pass. I made my way through the police lines to my studio and sat around numbly for most of the day. Outgoing communication was down and I was unable to respond to dozens of e-mail and phone messages wondering if we were all alive.

In the evening, I returned home and switched on television to learn the latest and to watch the riveting pornography of planes smashing over and over into buildings, ashamed at my own fascination. Commerce had also returned to the airwaves and the dour talk was again interrupted by commercials, happy faces commanding us to buy suv's and stock up on useless commodities.

Solidarity and civility had bloomed in the days following the attack as barriers of diffidence fell and comfort and information flowed freely between strangers. Acts of kindness and friendship multiplied and the public's demeanor became somber and respectful. We comforted each other with small exchanges of information, felt the powerful egalitarianism of disaster. The city's official response was magnificent, astonishing. Streets below 14th Street were closed to traffic and nobody but local residents was allowed in. The result was an eerie calm as people quietly took possession of the empty streets as after a big snowfall. The weather was mockingly beautiful and the city was, perversely, at its very best: quiet, free of cars, crisp, cooperative. When the wind shifted, though, the dreadful smell filled the air. And everywhere fell the ash.

Before Tuesday, thinking about what to write for this essay, for an issue about preservation, I had decided to lead with the opening of a new Issey Miyake boutique a block from my studio, designed by Frank Gehry, who, as chance would have it, I bumped into on Monday night — September 10 — while he inspected the frantic efforts to have the place in order for a party 48 hours hence. He asked me, with irony, whether I planned to shop there and I told him that what I really wanted was the return of the old natural foods market that had been driven out by the rise of prices in this now remorselessly fashionable neighborhood.

I had planned to respond to the narrowed focus among architects and critics in which "preservation" has been reduced to a battle of styles, an endless debate over modern building versus the historicism that serves as the official default for old neighborhoods like this one. The point I wanted to make was that the discussion had lost sight of the ecology of place, that we needed to preserve not simply the sense of visual reliability in beloved environments but also to be sensitive to the far more consequential issues of established ways of living, of daily habits, of the need for human permanence in chosen habitats.

Gehry's boutique was going to have been exhibit A because it was beautiful, the work of our most artistically accomplished architect. Now, confronted by the presence of the agonizing absence of the twin towers from our field of vision, I am thrown back into defending the role of architecture as an element of citizenship. Must it now be subsumed in the rhetoric of defiance and victory? Will we continue to look at architecture as the answer?

There has been a brave and understandable clamor for rebuilding. After all, this was a preeminent icon of the town and we don't want to give terror the symbolic victory of disfiguring our legendary skyline. Those terrorists — obviously informed about the structural character of this construction — used architecture as means of mass murder, and architecture was an accessory to the crime. The economic and narcissistic logics behind these towers caused a series of choices that simply put people at risk.

Risk assessment—like "threat" assessment for the military—is part of architecture. Among the risks the designers of the Trade Center decided were worthwhile was a one hour climb downstairs for people attempting to flee the upper stories of the building, impossible for the handicapped. Among the tradeoffs during construction was the elimination of asbestos fireproofing around the structural steel. There has been much discussion about whether the building—which sits along a primary approach route to La Guardia airport—was designed to survive the impact of a plane crash, and the answer circulated in the media was that yes, indeed, it had but of an older, smaller, aircraft of the vintage when the structure was designed. The question remains, though, about which harm's ways a building should be in.

I am uncertain about what should be done to heal the site. Perhaps this is the moment for a decisive break from the machismo of scale that foregrounds values of size and cost above all other signifiers of success and power. Perhaps this is the site for reimagining architecture, not from the position of either power or paranoia but from a sense of humanity and compassion. Perhaps, however, this is a site not to be rebuilt. I shudder at the trivial objects of memorial that will ultimately be offered, the ornamented isle amidst the gigantic new construction.

Perhaps this is a scar that should simply be left.

Perhaps the billions should be spent improving transportation and building in neglected parts of the city. Neglected parts of the world.

As the endless loop of planes crashing into buildings plays over and over in our heads, it is rapidly filed in the image bank of disasters: the the mushroom cloud over Hiroshima, the burning ships at Pearl Harbor, the ash-preserved figures of Pompeii. I had an especially icy feeling when I saw that first commercial on TV, the first interpolation of the rhetorical images of advertising between those of the disaster, assimilating the spectable to normal routines of capitalist visuality. Disaster morphed into a special effect. It's depressing how many interviewed refer to Bruce Willis, Independence Day, The Towering Inferno, the earthquake ride at Universal Studios.

But the tragedy has already invented its own memorial. On every lamppost and mailbox, fence and facade, thousands of images have been posted, photographs of the missing, advertising the ineradicable despair of their loved ones. All over the city, people stop and stare at these photographs taken when things were normal, formal portraits and tourist snaps, family photos, graduation pictures. We all look at them to see if we know their subjects, breathing with quiet relief when we don't but recognizing that every picture seems familiar. That every picture could have been our own or that of someone we love.

I am not chronically paranoid but I'm good and worried. Not so much about the next attack (though I am still afraid to fly) but about the reconstruction of our city and our culture. The victory for terror lies in our own frightened willingness to give up on the values that are under attack, values that lie at the core of what good architecture and urbanism are about: facilitating the face to face, creating places of privacy and personal sanctuary, accommodating the pleasures of community, foregrounding the beautiful.

Asked for an ID every morning by a guardsman in combat dress, listening to the President blustering about "smokin' them out of their holes, getting them running, and whipping them"—with the "them" as yet unknown—I fear for where we'll have to live from now on.

FIRST
RESPO

AS THE RECOVERY OPERATION PROGRESSED AND CLEARING OF THE SITE BECAME THE FOCUS OF ENERGY, WE WERE APPROACHED BY A LOCAL BUILDER TO SUGGEST A FORM OF TEMPORARY ENCLOSURE FOR THE SITE. This was meant to physically protect the public from the perilous process underway, to cordon the workplace from intrusion, and to—in some way—provide for the very large numbers of people who were pressing to visit Ground Zero.

Our initial proposal was for a large earthen berm to surround the site. Feeling that it was important to both secure and to mark the place, the enclosure took the form of a circular crater. This had obvious symbolism but also felt sufficiently substantial to preserve the site indefinitely as its use and design were discussed. Worried by the prospect of haste, we wanted to mark a place of reverence and deliberation, not to solve the "problem" of Ground Zero. With that in mind, we contemplated more durable materials for the project, including stone and brick as well as the possibility of looking into the void to be left at the site from the rim of the crater.

NSF

Convinced that the discussion of what should be done to recover the place had to exceed the limits of the site—extending not just to the rest of downtown but to the city as a whole—we also imagined that the temporary enclosure could have effects beyond Ground Zero. The initial notion was that it become a point of dissemination for greening and pedestrianization, for the healing ministrations of nature and for a network of human connections, leading both to and from the place of tragedy.

The Berm

Greenfill

THE
CENTER
CANNOT
HOLD

**IN HIS FAREWELL TO OFFICE, RUDY GIULIANI, STANDING IN ST. PAUL'S
CHAPEL — ADJACENT TO THE WORLD TRADE CENTER SITE — DECLARED,
"I REALLY BELIEVE WE SHOULDN'T THINK ABOUT THIS SITE OUT THERE,
RIGHT BEHIND US, RIGHT HERE, AS A SITE FOR ECONOMIC DEVELOP-
MENT.** We should think about a soaring, monumental, beautiful memorial that just draws millions of people here who just want to see it. We
have to be able to create something here that enshrines this forever and
that allows people to build on it and grow from it. And it's not going to
happen if we just think about it in a very narrow way."

Giuliani's speech reminded me of Eisenhower's leave-taking from
the presidency, in which he warned the nation against the growing
anti-democratic power of the "military-industrial complex." In both
cases, the cautionary appeals resonated because of their sources, one
from a military man and architect of the cold war, the other from a
mayor whose leadership favored planning by the "market."

Giuliani's heartfelt call for restraint ran counter to the business-as-
usual approach that has dominated official thinking since the tragedy.
This has included craven job-hunting by architects and robust talk
about responding to the terror by rapid rebuilding, bigger than ever.
The Lower Manhattan Redevelopment Corporation, empowered to decide the future of the site, is headed up by a patriarchal ex-director

of Goldman Sachs whose credibility seems untainted by the spectacle of his own firm migrating over the river to Jersey. With the exception of a single community representative, the board is comprised of the usual business crowd. Their initial consensus seems to favor the construction of a very large amount of office space on the cleared site of the fallen towers with the memorial simply a modest component. And rumors grind on about the working drawings already on the boards at Skidmore, Owings, and Merrill.

Fortunately, the competition for control over the site is both structural and complex. The Port Authority, Larry Silverstein (the ninety-nine year leaseholder), the Redevelopment Corporation, the federal, state, and city governments, survivor groups, the local community, the business improvement district, the Battery Park City Authority, the Transit Authority, and other civic and private interests are jostling to be heard and influential. If nothing else, this fog buys time for contention and for the serious consideration of alternatives.

What is clear is that despite the currently soft market, some of the 15 million square feet of lost space needs to replaced sooner rather than later and downtown's dysfunctions repaired to allow the city's economy to reestablish jobs and networks lost in the attack. And the eventual need is not simply for replacement space: the "Group of 35"—a business-heavy organization chaired by Charles Schumer and Robert Rubin—has predicted (in a report about the future of the city's commercial space) that an additional 60 million square feet of office space will be required by 2020.

The question is where to put it? Some will clearly go to lower Manhattan. The relationships that form the social and spatial substrate of commerce and culture downtown must be quickly reestablished by the restoration of infrastructure and the addition of new space. Railroading the restoration of the status quo by looking at the site as no more than its footprint, however, guarantees that we learn nothing from the tragedy and let the opportunity for better thinking slip away.

My studio is not far from the Western Union building at 60 Hudson Street, known to architects as the home of the New York City Building Department. Since September 11, this building has been the subject of unusual security, surrounded by concrete barriers and half a dozen police cars. It appears to be the only site outside the confines of Ground Zero to enjoy this level of fresh security, and the reason seems to be the building's longstanding role as the nexus both for telecommunications cables coming into New York City as well as trunk lines to the nation and the world, a logical next target for terror according to some scenarios.

A distributed, electronic system at the core of urban disaggregation depends on the joining of huge dispersed networks on a single site. The currently dominant pattern of our urbanism—enabled by the instantaneous proximity that the electronic web of phones, faxes, e-mails, and other global systems allow—is the rapid growth of the "edge city," a sprawling, non-place suburban realm that has become the antithesis of a traditional sense of place. It is the place to which security-conscious firms now feel increasingly impelled to retreat.

This growth is the result of more than new communications technology. The suburbs were fertilized by massive government intervention in highway construction, by radical tax policy, by shifts in the culture of desire, by racism, by cheap, unencumbered land, and by an earlier fear of terror. The prospect of nuclear annihilation that made urban concentrations particularly vulnerable was on the minds of many planners during the cold war, both in the U.S. and abroad. This massive de-urbanization in Maoist China was the direct result of nuclear anxiety. The dispersal facilitated by the Interstates—our erstwhile "National Defense Highway"—was likewise more than simply good for General Motors: both the company and the U.S. were playing at the same stratego-urban games.

Whatever the causes, however, the effects of this pattern of urbanization were in many ways antithetical to the presumptions behind the space of lower Manhattan and its kith. Here, concentration has long been considered crucially advantageous. The possibility of conducting economic affairs face to face, the collective housing of related bureaucracies and businesses (the famous FIRE sectors that make up the majority of business downtown), the dense life of the streets, the convenience of having everything at hand, are the material basis for the viability of the main financial district for the planet. Its characteristic form—the superimpostion of skyscrapers on the medieval street pattern left by the

Dutch — has given downtown its indelible shape.

Any changes reconstruction brings must deepen this formal singularity, expand the possibilities of exchange, and broaden the mix of uses supported. While it is now a bromide to apologize before suggesting that the tragedy can be turned to advantage, have positive consequences, we must find a way to make things better. Life downtown is going to be refounded, and the imperative is to do it well. In fact, the enormous disruption in the life of the city has already had a number of constructive effects. Traffic is dramatically reduced on local streets, the polluted sewer of Canal Street is suddenly tractable, and the emergency carpooling and limited access instituted as the result of the disaster are important contributions to a sustainable urban ecology.

The radical act of the terrorists opens a space for us to think radically as well, to examine alternatives for the future of all of New York City. It is no coincidence that we have constructed a skyline in the image of a bar graph. This is not simply an abstraction but an utterly simple means of multiplying wealth: where land is scarce, make more. Lots more. There is a fantasy of Manhattan as driven by a pure and perpetual increase in density. But while our dynamism is surely a product of critical mass, all arguments for concentration are not the same. Viewed from the perspective of the city as a whole, the hyperconcentration of the Trade Center was not necessarily optimal by any standard other than profit, and even that proved elusive.

Density has a downside in over-crowding and strained services, but this is not necessarily the result the hyper-scale of any particular building. More critical than specific effects on the ground are the consequences for densities elsewhere. While the anxiety over corporate and population flight to the suburbs comes from a general fear of both economic and social losses, the all-eggs-in-one-basket approach slights other areas of the city themselves in need of jobs, construction, and greater concentration. Manhattan's gain has been the boroughs' loss: the rise of the island's office towers historically marks the decline of industrial employment throughout the city and has obliged the respiratory pattern of one-directional commuting of the contemporary city. A new form of producing wealth with new spatial requirements has — over the century — completely supplanted its predecessor.

With thousands of jobs already relocated out of the city, a solution to the "practical" problems of reconstruction can and must engage possibilities well beyond the confines of the downtown site. While the billions that will be available for new building—from insurance, from federal aid, from city coffers, from developers—are certainly needed to restore health to the enterprises formerly in or servicing the Trade Center, it seems reasonable to question—given the probable level of this investment—whether such massive expenditure should be focused exclusively here rather than throughout the city at additional sites of need and opportunity, places development could transform.

The majority of the New York City's population and geography is not in Manhattan: the island comprises only 8% of the city's land area and 19% of its inhabitants. According to the 2000 census, the residential growth of the island since 1990—slightly over 3%—lags far behind the explosive growth of Staten Island (17%) and Queens (nearly 15%), and dramatic increases in the Bronx (10.7%) and Brooklyn (7.2%). Manhattan, however, remains the city's economic engine, producing 67% of its jobs and 46% of its retail sales.

These imbalances have fundamentally reshaped the city. The great infusions of capital and the artificial fortunes of the last decade have propelled the price of real estate in much of Manhattan to the stratosphere, accelerating the flight of the middle class and the poor and making the borough increasingly monochrome. We continue to revere our island as a place of thick, urbane interaction and cling to the fantasy of the great mixing engine of difference, of a place with many quarters housing many kinds of people. Increasingly, however, the differences in Manhattan's neighborhoods are merely physical. This uneven development and accelerated metamorphosis have had dramatic effects, distorting the character of our urbanity decisively.

Here in Tribeca, we are at the end of a familiar cycle in which a neighborhood moves from a mix of warehouses, manufacturing, offices, and housing, to an "artistic" neighborhood, and now to the climax form of gentrification, an extreme high-end residential district. The corollary is that the jobs and people formerly employed here have either been eliminated or moved elsewhere: to the Hunt's Point Market in the Bronx, to low-wage environments offshore, to the suburbs, or to the new bohemias of Williamsburg or Long Island City. We have scrupulously preserved the architectural character of Tribeca but at the expense of its human character.

With the exception of Chinatown, Manhattan south of 110th Street has become a faded mosaic of former ethnic enclaves and cultural variety. Increasingly, the city's ethnic and cultural quarters are being solidified outside the borough, in Flushing, Greenpoint, DUMBO, or along Atlantic Avenue. Although the city remains a beacon for immigrants — both from abroad and from home — the sites of intake and expression are not what they were, but have been preserved to death. Manhattan is ceasing to be a place to get a start and becoming inhospitable to striving, less and less like New York.

But big changes can also suggest big opportunities for burgeoning neighborhoods struggling to find form or merely to keep up. Not all disaggregation leads to sprawl. Better, perhaps, to call it reaggregation, but it is also a notion that can be useful in cultivating character and encouraging development within more traditional, compact, cities like New York, itself the central place for an enormous region. The point is not to make New York more like Phoenix or Los Angeles but to make the city as a whole more like New York.

Because of its dynamic population and superb movement infrastructure, New York City can become a model of a new kind of polycentric metropolis with Manhattan remaining its *centro di tutti centri*, its concentrated vitality unsapped. In fact, Manhattan is itself already polycentric: the disaggregation represented by, for example, the easy movement of financial and legal services firms from downtown to midtown in recent years suggests that there is a certain fluidity to the idea of proximity within the city, that convenient movement and strong local character can substitute for immediate adjacency within an overall context of density.

Reinforcing New York's special polycentricity would return the city to something of its pre-20th century character by restoring a network of autonomous, comprehensible places. Such a "village" structure — the origin of the great city of variegated neighborhoods — is again made possible by the technology behind the ephemeral and flexible nets and flows of the 21st. Because it is aspatial, this malleability need not simply lead to generic sprawl but can fit within—and reinforce—any preexisting infrastructure of neighborhood differences.

Cultivating this "natural" polycentricity would multiply opportunities for more self-sufficient neighborhoods where people walk to work, to school, to recreation, and to culture. Such places would satisfy many of the needs that impel people to seek the densities and economies of suburbs and edge cities. By regenerating local character, the energy of intra-city reaggregation could reinforce the expressive singularity of each of the neighborhoods to which its energies were applied—the Asian flavor of Flushing, the Latin American atmosphere of the Bronx Hub, the African cultures of Harlem.

This would be an advance on the wing-and-a-prayer style of current planning in which good intentions are simultaneously frustrated by imprecise plans and the absence of economic drivers to set them in motion before changing times render them irrelevant. By joining physical planning to direct investment and to zoning and economic incentives, we can redistribute uses to a set of centers outside Manhattan where land and transit connections are available and economical, places like Flushing, Jamaica, Queens Plaza, Sunnyside the Bronx Hub, St. George, and Downtown Brooklyn, among others. These sites—also identified in the report of the Group of 35—are not mysterious either in their needs or their suitability.

Planning comprehensively could help assure the mixed-use character of these places by including residential construction matched to the numbers of new workplaces, a pattern that has already begun downtown where substantial office space has actually been eliminated by conversion to residential use. Indeed, in the last ten years 40 office buildings have been converted to residential use downtown, part of an 18% population growth in the area below Canal Street. The sense of locality that grows from a well-finessed mix would be further reinforced by the decentralization of cultural growth (the City Opera, the Guggenheim, the Whitney, the Met and the Jets are all seeking space) and by encouraging the development of new cultural, health care, educational, and commercial institutions to enhance the variety and life of these neighborhood centers.

It is critical, however, that these centers be envisioned and planned as semi-autonomous and not simply as ancillary. Downtown Brooklyn is already one of the largest "central places" in America but continues to be thought of as a back-office for Manhattan. The key is zoning for sustainability and difference, not simply for a series of mini-Manhattans. Although the skyscraper is a preeminent symbol of 20th century technology and of the culture of the corporation, other paradigms must now emerge as values change. The economic driver that has impelled these heights will be usefully moderated in smaller centers which foreground strong environmental values and in which land prices are restrainedly low.

Downtown Manhattan is the commercial district with the highest public transportation usage in the country. 85% of those who come to work there — 350,000 people a day — arrive on mass transit. A comprehensive re-examination and reinforcement of this pattern is crucial to sustaining the city but must be approached non-centrifugally to facilitate movement not simply in and out of Manhattan but between the developing centers of lived life, reinforcing the repatterning. Our waterways, in particular, offer a tremendous opportunity for creating such links with great economy. In addition, the city's large areas of public greenspace and municipally owned property can be used to begin to create a third transport net — for pedestrians, bikers, and non-aggressive zero-emissions vehicles — to supplement the street grid and the subway.

Business-as-usual in New York City is more than the compulsion to repeat patterns of the past: our talent is creating the new. In the case of downtown Manhattan, however, it is also important to recognize that this is an area of the city that is near completion, its project of build-out and of formal invention almost done. The construction of the World Trade Center, the isolation of Battery Park City by an overwide highway, the nasty scale of many newer high-rises, the abandonment of the piers, the elimination of manufacturing and small-scale commercial activity, and the elevation of the East Side highway are all assaults on a satisfying paradigm of great scale contrasts, rich architectural textures, and pedestrian primacy that lies at the core of what's best about downtown. Restoring this is the task at hand and it cannot be accomplished in Lower Manhattan alone.

A PLA

FOR

CONVINCED THAT IT WAS FAR TOO EARLY TO BEGIN TO THINK ABOUT WHAT ACTIVITIES SHOULD RETURN TO GROUND ZERO, OUR EARLY STUDIES LOOKED BEYOND THE SITE. This was not simply a question of protecting a space of mourning but of answering the array of aspirations that arose in the aftermath of the tragedy—for office and commercial space, for transit improvements, for housing, for civic institutions, for green space, and, above all for a suitable memorial to September 11. These not simply exceeded the bearing capacity of those fraught fourteen acres, they affronted the dead, still entombed there.

We therefore began to look both at ways in which lost functions could be restored elsewhere. The project initially took the form of a series of studies of the possibilities for a disaggregated, distributed strategy for replacing lost space and jobs. This became the basis for a design studio at City College that looked at the possibility of building a million square feet of office and commercial space, 2500 housing units, and a major cultural facility in each of half a dozen outlying city neighborhoods. The logic of this idea grew not simply from a sense of ethical restraint but also from the observation that displaced businesses were quickly re-housed and still left many millions of square feet of office space vacant downtown. A subsequent study found an "easy" additional ten million square feet in soft and vacant sites in the immediate vicinity of Ground Zero.

Assured that there was no immediate shortage of replacement space, we prepared a more comprehensive plan for Lower Manhattan that left the specific use of the site undetermined. The plan — river to river below Canal Street — comprises a number of major interventions, all of which answer needs that were present before 9/11.

→ Burial of West Street / South Street from the Holland Tunnel to the Manhattan Bridge and the use of the newly created ground above for public green and recreational space.

→ Rerouting of cross town traffic from the Holland Tunnel to the Manhattan Bridge through the new tunnel.

→ Burial of the approaches to the Brooklyn Battery Tunnel and the use of newly created ground above for development and a greensward linked to Battery Park.

→ Creation of an academic campus comprising Borough of Manhattan Community College, St. John's University, Stuyvesant High School, the new lower Manhattan High School, PS/IS 89, and PS 284.

→ Use of Ground Zero as a point of dissemination for widespread pedestrianization and greening in lower Manhattan.

→ Replacement of lost space by the build-out of soft and vacant sites for mixed use, including the possibility of constructing housing on piers.

→ An intermodal World Transportation Center at and around Ground Zero, including new lines for the LIRR and Second Avenue Subway, a light-rail system running north to the Javits Center, Penn Station, Port Authority, and Grand Central, a commuter bus terminal, and direct rail and ferry connections to JFK and Newark.

→ Additional landfill north of Battery Park City to solve existing hydrological problems and to create additional park and recreational space.

REPLACING LOST SPACE

Fortunately, necessity moots the question. In Lower Manhattan, every fifth floor of office space is empty. If nothing else, this high vacancy rate provides both shelter from demand as well as time for a more broadly based consideration of the distribution of such space in the future. We suggest three possible strategies for constructing replacement space off Ground Zero. We do not specify the uses for these sites but feel strongly that the future of downtown lies in maximizing the mix to produce a true "24 hour" community.

REGIONAL DISAGGREGATION

New York City is blessed with a number of centers that are currently capable of absorbing several million square feet of office construction. Each of these centers has strong transportation links, a nearby population of potential employees, very particular local character, and pressing economic needs. The distribution of new office space in these neighborhoods would be wise from the standpoint of local development, of transportation, and of the environment.

LOCAL DISAGGREGATION

The space lost in the disaster might also be replaced on a variety of locations below Canal Street. Not simply is vacant office space abundant, more than enough land currently exists (or would be created by a variety of the schemes currently under discussion) to rebuild what has been lost. Indeed, given the diverse character of the tenancy of the Trade Center, there is no strong argument for repeating its massive concentration other than maximizing the economic return of the site itself.

An easy 10 million square feet

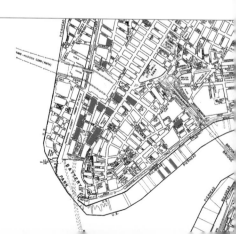

YANKEE STADIUM
BRONX HUB

125TH ST.

FLUSHING

QUEENS PLAZA
SUNNYSIDE

JAMAICA

DOWNTOWN
BROOKLYN

ST. GEORGE

Distributed Growth

A PLAN FOR DOWNTOWN
NOVEMBER 2001

THE TRIPLE SWITCH

Two sites in south midtown are currently the focus of considerable municipal and private speculation. The area around the Javits Center and the block currently used for Madison Square Garden and its adjoining office tower could be utilized to build well over 10 million square feet of space. The economic logic of such a relocation might be enhanced by a broader redistribution of uses. Under such a strategy, Madison Square Garden might move to the vicinity of Ground Zero or to the West Side Rail Yards and the proposed expansion of the Javits Center might be achieved, in part, by building components both downtown and above Penn Station. While this would not satisfy the requirements of extremely large exhibitions, it would expand the capacity of Javits to conduct many events simultaneously. It might also allow a kind of specialization, with the spun-off component treated as a forum for large scale public meetings and performances.

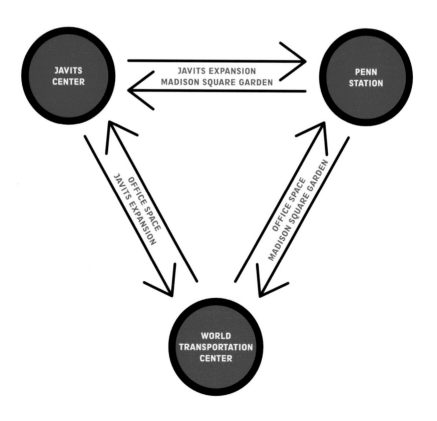

DOWNTOWN CULTURE

New housing, new commercial space, and new cultural and civic institutions must be added to the mix.

→ The Museum of the City of New York
→ The Municipal Archives
→ A Museum of 9/11
→ An Institute of Peace and Tolerance
→ The New York City Opera
→ A Dance Theater Complex
→ A Center for Non-Profit Arts Organizations
→ The New Lower Manhattan High School
→ The Guggenheim Museum
→ An Arab-American Museum
→ The Fire Department Museum
→ The Skyscraper Museum
→ A Center for NGO's
→ United Nations Offices
→ The New York Historical Society
→ A School of World Music
→ A School of Languages
→ An Elementary School
→ A Branch of the Metropolitan Museum
→ A Chinese Museum and Cultural Center
→ An Institute of Building Safety
→ An Institute of Urban Sustainability
→ A Support Center for Survivors and Victims
→ The Architectural League
→ A Center for Dialogue Among Religions

THE WORLD TRANSPORTATION CENTER

85% of the people who work in lower Manhattan commute by public transportation, the highest rate in the country. Reinforcing this pattern will bring vitality to the area and will dramatically increase its environmental sustainability. We support major upgrades in the transit infrastructure downtown, including the following:

1 Construction of an intermodal transit center uniting all means and lines in a single, sheltered environment.

2 Construction of link with the Long Island Railroad via a new East River Tunnel.

3 Completion of the Second Avenue Subway to serve the site.

4 Creation of direct links to Newark Airport (via an extension of the Path) and to Kennedy (via the IND, the LIRR, the Airtrain, and fast ferries).

5 Extension of Metro-North to the site.

6 Construction of a West Side light-rail line to link the World Transportation Center, the Javits Center, Penn Station, the Port Authority, and Grand Central.

7 Dramatic extension of ferry service, especially along the two coasts of Manhattan and between the boroughs.

8 Great increases in the space reserved for pedestrians and bikers throughout downtown.

9 A bus station for regional commuters.

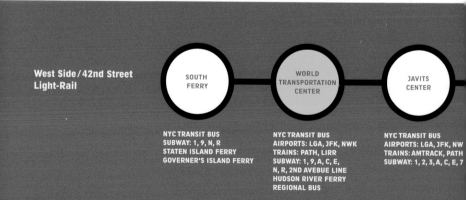

West Side/42nd Street Light-Rail

SOUTH FERRY

WORLD TRANSPORTATION CENTER

JAVITS CENTER

NYC TRANSIT BUS
SUBWAY: 1, 9, N, R
STATEN ISLAND FERRY
GOVERNER'S ISLAND FERRY

NYC TRANSIT BUS
AIRPORTS: LGA, JFK, NWK
TRAINS: PATH, LIRR
SUBWAY: 1, 9, A, C, E,
N, R, 2ND AVEBUE LINE
HUDSON RIVER FERRY
REGIONAL BUS

NYC TRANSIT BUS
AIRPORTS: LGA, JFK, NW
TRAINS: AMTRACK, PATH
SUBWAY: 1, 2, 3, A, C, E, 7

1,9 TO RIVERDALE, THE BRONX

A TO INWOOD, MANHATTAN
E TO JAMAICA, QUEENS

4,5,6 TO THE BRONX

WEST SIDE LIGHT RAIL

FERRIES

J,Z TO JAMAICA, QUEENS
M TO MIDDLE VILLAGE, QUEENS

2ND AVENUE SUBWAY

J TRANSIT/PATH
O NEWARK &
OBOKEN, NJ

LIRR TO BROOKLYN/QUEENS

A,C TO WOODHAVEN / FAR ROCKAWAY, BROOKLYN
JFK AIRPORT

1,9 TO SOUTH FERRY

2 TO FLATBUSH, BROOKLYN
3 TO EAST NEW YORK, BROOKLYN

J,Z TO BAY PARKWAY, BROOKLYN

5 TO FLATBUSH, BROOKLYN

Transit Concourse

PENN STATION MADISON SQUARE GARDEN	PORT AUTHORITY BUS TERMINAL	GRAND CENTRAL TERMINAL	UNITED NATIONS
NYC TRANSIT BUS AIRPORTS: LGA, JFK, NWK TRAINS: PATH, LIRR SUBWAY: 1, 2, 3, A, C, E, 7 HUDSON RIVER FERRY	NYC TRANSIT BUS AIRPORTS: NWK TRAINS: PATH SUBWAY: A, C, E, 7	NYC TRANSIT BUS AIRPORTS: LGA, JFK TRAINS: AMTRACK SUBWAY: 4, 5, 6, 7, S	NYC TRANSIT BUS EAST RIVER FERRY

A PLAN FOR DOWNTOWN
NOVEMBER 2001

DOWNTOWN CAMPUS

The collection of educational institutuions at the western end of Chambers Street offers an opportunity for great synergistic development. The most minimal version of the West Street tunnel currently being discussed would allow the creation of a continuous campus embracing institutions including Borough of Manhattan Community College, Stuyvesant High School, an intermediate school, and two grade schools, St. John's University, the CUNY Center for Worker Education, and the new Lower Manhattan High School. This diagram shows a schematic version of such a plan in which a series of shared quadrangles and sports facilities provide the glue to bind these schools into a single place. The superb riverside site and abundant green space could offer a wonderful atmosphere for cooperative learning.

HYDROLOGIC FILL

The squared off north end of Battery Park City creates an environmental dead zone, prevented by its geometry from conducing appropriate flushing action. A recontouring of the site by additional landfill would both remedy this hydrological problem and provide additional park and recreational space in a part of town that is severely lacking in both.

GREEN LINES

Recovered from the language of diplomacy, "green lines" are diagrammatic indications of nets and routes that would be taken from the automotive system and returned to people on foot. Streets would either be fully pedestrianized or be reduced in dimension as greenfill replaced lanes of traffic. This would provide both new walking and greenspace but would also permit the development of new activities proper to the public realm, including waste-management sites, cafes, bicycle sheds, and so on. Such greenfill might extend throughout the city, using downtown as a point of connection of simply as a model.

GREAT LAWN

Should West Street be buried all the way to the Battery Tunnel, the opportunity arises to eliminate the exit and entry ramps that currently occupy several pivotal blocks downtown. We propose that the blocks

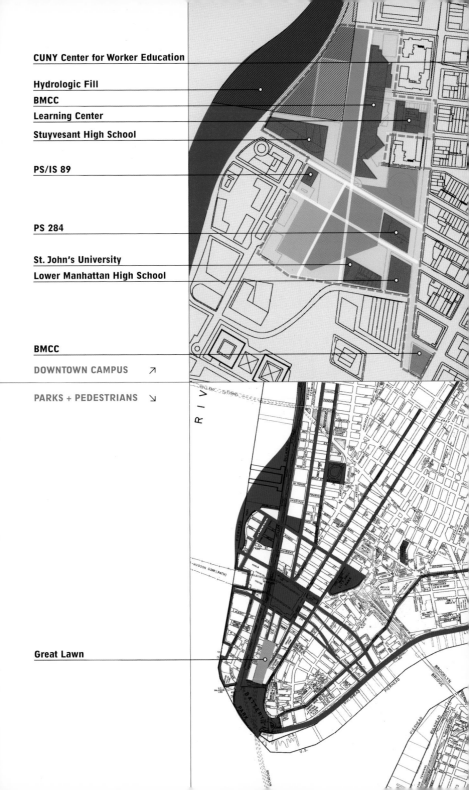

CUNY Center for Worker Education

Hydrologic Fill

BMCC

Learning Center

Stuyvesant High School

PS/IS 89

PS 284

St. John's University

Lower Manhattan High School

BMCC

DOWNTOWN CAMPUS ↗

PARKS + PEDESTRIANS ↘

Great Lawn

south of Rector Street now occupied by automotive uses on either side of the line of Washington Street between Trinity and West Streets become a great lawn extending to Battery Park, lined by new building. This miniature Central Park would add views and value to the construction surrounding it and offer a number of sites for replacing space lost at Ground Zero.

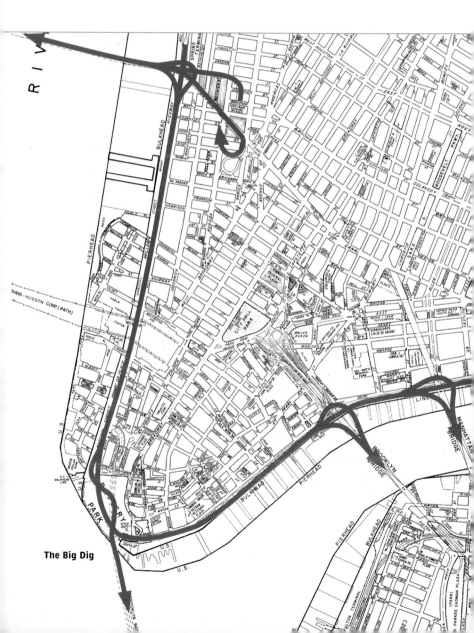

The Big Dig

A PLAN FOR DOWNTOWN
NOVEMBER 2001

A PLAN FOR DOWNTOWN

New Green Space

Existing Green Space

New Construction

Pedestrian Enhancements

Civic Buildings

Hydrologic Fill

SIX MONTHS

DURING THE WEEK OF THE SIX-MONTH ANNIVERSARY OF THE TRADE CENTER ATTACK, I WALKED DOWN TO SEE THE TOWERS OF LIGHT ON A FOGGY EVENING. The clouds lay low and their effect was startling and dramatic, occluding and revealing the powerful skyward beams, shrouding downtown in an otherworldly glow. It was completely beautiful and a little frightening, a genuinely artistic sublimity that could be taken for what it was, a feeling quite different from the embarrassed awe that shamed earlier fascinations with the twisted, mesmerizing rubble at Ground Zero.

The site is now nearly clear, thanks to the grim, selfless energy of those laboring there round the clock. As workers reach the bottom of the pile, they are discovering the remains of comrades trapped on lower floors and in the lobby when the towers collapsed. The two shafts of light seem completely apt at this moment of transition from removal and recovery to the consideration of what is to come. They assert the possibility of a memorial of both power and presence, and set a high standard for future projects. That they are there at all also demonstrates the power of the informal consensus that has, for better and worse, begun to determine what can and cannot happen on this place.

For the moment, we find ourselves in a curious interregnum downtown. While no plans have been finalized, there has been intense jockeying for position, both publicly and, especially, behind the scenes. With the formation of the Lower Manhattan Development Corporation, planning responsibility has, however, become clearer, even if the actual power to undertake construction remains dispersed and uncertain. The site is owned by the Port Authority (controlled by the governors of New York and New Jersey), sits within the City of New York, is laced with transport and utility infrastructure controlled by various agencies, and has been leased to Larry Silverstein—a New York real estate mogul with particularly dreary architectural sensibilities (four 50-story towers on the site was his initial public suggestion)—and to Westfield, an Australian shopping-mall management company that was to have run the huge retail complex beneath the towers.

In addition to these legal stakeholders, the public has made its sentiments known through both traditional political activities and a welter of self-organized alliances that have been meeting regularly and working hard to promulgate ideas for reconstruction. One of the most broad-based of these coalitions—New York/New Visions—recently released a preliminary report that includes a variety of sensible findings, most crucially a call to look beyond the immediate site of the towers and consider the planning of downtown Manhattan as a whole. The report recognizes an historic opportunity to reattach Battery Park City to the island from which it has long been isolated, to increase pedestrian links, to unify and augment a series of transit lines that converge but don't quite meet at the site, and to intensify the mix of uses in the area. And they are not alone; the outpouring of proposals and opinions has been bracing: At no time in my memory can I recall so many discussing questions of planning and urbanism so fervently.

As I write this, the LMDC has just released its first statement of principles for the "future of Lower Manhattan" and its board—appointed during the Giuliani administration—has been expanded to include four directors chosen by Mayor Bloomberg. These are Billie Tsien, the first designer named, Carl Weisbrod, the head of the downtown business improvement district, E. Stanley O'Neal, the president of Merrill Lynch, and Sally Hernandez-Pinero, a deputy mayor in the Dinkins administration. The mayor has clearly sent a message about diversity by placing Asian-, African-, and Hispanic-Americans—among them two women—on a board hitherto dominated by white, male plutocrats and bureaucrats.

The new principles have been honchoed by Alex Garvin, recently hired as the LMDC's vice president for planning. New York City planning commissioner, professor at the Yale School of Architecture, and author of the ingenious and politically adroit proposal for the 2012 Olympics (done for Daniel Doctoroff, now deputy mayor for economic development and a major player downtown), Garvin has articulated a framework that is both reasonable and very canny. Clearly, Garvin has been listening carefully, and his initial recommendations parallel those emerging from the broader community of interests. The importance of the memorial is foregrounded, infrastructure and transportation are emphasized, mixed use is invoked, pedestrianism encouraged, open space celebrated, and environmentalism tithed.

These principles are sound and should attract wide support. However, they are strategic in their avoidance of the more controversial aspects of the plan that must finally emerge. The two big issues are who decides the fate of the site and what is actually to be done at Ground Zero. While the report and the new appointments may reassure the public about decisions many feared would be reached behind closed doors, the principles do not take a definitive position on the future of the site itself, listing but not locating uses and calling for a lot of work to take place underground. This reticence is appropriate at this stage: there is still plenty of time to get it right.

The closest the principles come to a translatable declaration of design intent is in their call for the restoration of "all or a portion of" the street grid obliterated by the construction of the Trade Center. However, the plan specifically mentions only two streets that cross the site—Greenwich Street, running north-south and Fulton Street, running east-west—not the 12 blocks that originally stood there. Of course, an open space or memorial scheme (or, for that matter, a commercial, mixed-use development) could establish cross-site connections without restoring the grid as such. The question, therefore, remains whether there will be a block scheme for the site—defining a series of clear development parcels—or some other approach.

Today—the day after the release of the LMDC's principles—

Silverstein revealed his plans for the first site to be put in play, the former 7 WTC (which collapsed a few hours after the twin towers with, miraculously, no loss of life) The site is pivotal both because it holds an electric substation that must be replaced expeditiously and because the earlier building had eliminated Greenwich Street, which virtually everyone now agrees should be unblocked. In the just publised diagram of the scheme developed for Silverstein by David Childs of Skidmore, Owings, and Merrill, the missing block of Greenwich has been restored with the result that the footprint of the new building is considerably smaller than the original. Although the new tower will be higher than its predecessor, there is a net reduction of 300,000 square feet of space.

This begs the question of what will be done with the leftover development rights, and rumors are flying that Silverstein is deep in renegotiating the terms of his lease with the Port Authority to reflect the diminished carrying capacity of the site. It has also been suggested that this may simply be the beginning of a much more protracted negotiation, to escape any financial liability from the potential consequences of the "official" plan. Indeed, rumors are also circulating that SOM is preparing studies for the entire WTC site on Silverstein's behalf as part of his strategic negotiation for a new lease.

SOM has been ubiquitous downtown. Marilyn Taylor, chairman of the firm, has emerged as a key exponent of the New Visions report and is also leading a planning study of lower Manhattan's east side funded by Weisbrod's Downtown Alliance, while Childs is designing 7 WTC and doing planning studies for Silverstein. Am I overreacting to the hydra of an interlocking architectural/developer directorate or to the fact that all the commissions doled out thus far have gone to one firm? There is a giant potential conflict between business and citizenship here, and SOM needs to lay its cards on the table vis a vis its own desires and interests for Ground Zero.

The real wild card in all of this, though, is the memorial. In recent weeks I've gotten the strong sense that the idea that the entire site be dedicated to commemoration is being quietly slipped off the table. Most vocal among the supporters of such a plan have been the tragedy's bereaved survivors, although this is not a uniform position among them. This community has been deeply disappointed at being excluded from representation on the LMDC, and at having been offered a role only in its memorial subcommittee. Advocates (myself included) for leaving most of this sacral site open as a civic, memorial, space seem to be increasingly marginalized. I get the impression that the "cooler heads" in power regard any such scheme as the victory of sentiment over reason (i.e., money) and that the dispassionate, "rational" position is for a mix of economic, cultural, and memorial activities on the site.

There is no purely logical method for adjudicating these conflicting claims. In the absence of genuinely competing plans, developed as actual designs, there cannot be a basis for deciding on the superiority of one solution over another. It would be a shame if the process were to proceed "deductively" as if the solution could simply be programmed by consensus. Eventually, there is sure to be a competition for some portion of the site, something specifically designated as the memorial. But the time to throw the process open is now. With a good, comprehensive set of ideas on the table, it is critical that the process engage a wide range of alternatives. The need now is for *formal* arguments that interpret the consensus artistically, fertilizing the process with invention.

Walking around the almost completely cleared site the other day, I was struck both by the agonizing extent of the void and its profound legibility. In visual and urbanistic terms, this is not a space that must be built upon to find its compelling visual, functional, and expressive logics. It is too soon to close this possibility down.

THINKING
INSIDE
THE
BOX

ADMITTEDLY, I WENT TO THE JULY 20 "LISTENING TO THE CITY" MEETING AT THE JAVITS CENTER WITH VISIONS OF MYSELF AS THAT WOMAN IN THE LEGENDARY MACINTOSH COMMERCIAL, RUNNING THROUGH AN AUDTIORIUM OF PASSIVE PLEBS TO HURL HER HAMMER AT THE MONSTER SCREEN ON WHICH BIG BROTHER BLUE WAS PROCLAIMING WHAT A FINE AND ORDERLY PLACE THE ORWELLIAN WORLD WAS. The set-up seemed to confirm my worst fears for the event: 5,000 people randomly assigned to 500 tables, watching speakers and images on giant video screens, each of us equipped with a remote control key pad for "voting," every table with a volunteer "facilitator" (ours a German from Toronto), and with a laptop on which to communicate with a team of compilers who would determine opinion trends across the room.

No more reassuring was the parade of the usual white men—from the Port Authority, the Lower Manhattan Development Corporation, the city government and the Regional Plan Association—who extolled the importance of the process and presented the famous six schemes compiled by the LMDC and its consultants. The working portion of the event was conducted by Carolyn Lukensmeyer, a professional facilitator—who combined many of the more annoying aspects of Oprah and Kim Il Sung. Indeed, as the meeting wore on, I increasingly felt like a delegate to a 1950's Soviet Party Congress: the Central Committee has carefully selected this list of identical candidates for your consideration (in this case, the six schemes for street grids, office, shopping, hotel, memorial, and transit complexes): you may now vote. My own strained ability to participate in well-behaved Nielson-family fashion finally evaporated when Lukensmeyer ("give yourselves a nice round of applause") embellished her script with a brief pep talk on how the meeting was democratic as all get out because, "in democracy, the people have a chance to speak!" Seizing upon this right, I rose to my feet to shout "Buuuulllllshiiiit! Democracy means the people have the power to choose!"

This tiny act of insurrection went almost completely unnoticed. Inaudible over the amplified pronouncements being broadcast from the stage and invisible in the vast hall and crowd, my outburst attracted a smattering of applause from nearby tables and not the slightest notice from anyone else. Not the first time for me, but telling nonetheless. The charade of "electronic democracy" was burst by the asymmetries of power in that room, the careful control of both agenda and process from above. Like most planning, decision-making belonged to the powerful, reaction to the people. At the Javits Center, original ideas were excluded because they—naturally—lacked a constituency: all the opinions that we wrote on our computer were vetted to see if enough people *already* shared them to have them played back to the audience. Creativity thus foreclosed by stifling the new or the unusual and by total control of what could be discussed. For example, there was not even the mention among the alleged "choices" of a scheme that would preserve the entire site as a memorial.

But something strongly constructive nevertheless happened at the meeting and in its aftermath. This had nothing to do with changing the underlying institutional structures—the virtually unaccountable quasi-governmental agencies—that are running the process but with the clarity of the audience response to the uninspiring goods on offer. Emerging from the self-congratulatory and coercive process was a genuine act of protest: the audience clearly exercised the one planning power that's left in the hands of citizens, the power to say no. Given the opportunity to vote scheme-by-scheme, the crowd offered a pox on all houses, refusing enthusiasm for any of the big plans.

Power had certainly anticipated this. Indeed, no sooner had Beyer Blinder Belle—the firm chosen to produce the six "alternatives"—revealed the schemes during the week preceding the big meeting than a fusillade of gunfire rained on them from every direction. Even John Whitehead, chairman and patriarch of the LMDC, mumbled with embarrassment about this being "only a beginning" at the press conference at which his misshapen offspring were first presented. Likewise, the Mayor (who has recently called for the inclusion of housing on the site), the media (including Paul Goldberger, Ada Louise Huxtable, and Herbert Muschamp), and the person in the street responded with a raucous ho-hum. Even the governor (up for reelection in November and the man with far and away the most power to influence the course of events) came out firmly for the preservation of the footprints of the towers and argued for a design that looks beyond the limits of the site. And, in the post-Enron environment, there is a growing sense that the leaders of the development community may not be the most dedicated keepers of the commonweal and that their plan to restore business-as-usual intolerably ignores both ethical and civic values.

The dreadful work presented in this first round was not simply a product of failed democracy, the avarice of power, and programming that grew primarily from the imperative to make money; the design process was flawed conceptually. Democracy, after all, has only a tenuous relationship to great art and a vote cannot create it, only sanction it. The real problem with this (non-democratic) process is its acceptance of one of the cherished myths of modernity—that planning is essentially a rational, objective, procedure, that a "correct" solution can be derived by a hard-headed look at the facts. This allows a false distinction to be made between planning (something on which all reasonable people should be able to agree) and architecture (the fickle realm of taste). By representing the six proposals as planning (this was not architecture, we were endlessly told, despite what we could plainly see were buildings, parks, streets, and squares), the LMDC covered its ass by acting as if the most fundamental issues of form, organization, and character were simply the outgrowth of logical thinking.

The mediocrity of the results so far is also attributable to the mindset of those designers to whom this project has been entrusted.

Although Alex Garvin, the head of planning for the LMDC, is knowledgeable, dedicated, and politically skilled, he has no track record as a friend of the imagination. Ideologically, he is squarely in the Andres Duany wing of the New Urbanist camp, and his vision appears hemmed by his traditionalist sensibility. Morevover, every architectural firm "officially" working on the site shares this proclivity. And a remarkably supine group of professionals they are: no one from within any of the architectural firms or official bodies involved in the process has publicly spoken out for a change in the office building program, for a more far-reaching planning process, or for a competition.

Real decisions continue to be made behind the scenes, without formal accountability, despite the pretense. This same impropriety characterizes the LMDC's design process and style of inclusion. Beyer Blinder Belle was allegedly chosen as the site designers through an "open" RFP and stand to make a fee of something over $1 million (out of a total contract of $3 million). But to call the RFP open is like staying that Trump Plaza is open to anyone who wants to live there. The LMDC's RFP —which attracted only 15 proposals—was carefully restricted by a requirement that each firm have worked on at least three $100 million projects, assuring that only very large corporate offices would be eligible. At the same time the RFP was proceeding, however, three other firms were working away semi-officially without having gone through any public process at all, save favoritism. SOM, Larry Silverstein's architect, was producing plans for the site. Cooper, Robertson was master planning on behalf of Brookfield Properties, owners of the World Financial Center and lessors of the destoryed shopping mall. And Peterson/Littenberg (a very small firm that would never have qualified via the official process) was hired by the LMDC to be its "in-house" design consultants. This particular choice was presumably based on long personal association with Alex Garvin, deriving from shared traditionalist taste and collegial days at the Yale architectural school (whose current dean, the neo-con guru Robert Stern, was one of the six on the LMDC short list).

In the run-up to designating the six schemes for the public presentation, the LMDC looked at nine plans from Beyer Blinder Belle and two from Peterson/Littenberg as well as at the plans commissioned by

Brookfield and Silverstein. The board members then voted to select two of the Beyer Blinder Belle plans, two from Peterson/Littenberg and one each from Cooper, Roberston and SOM. This choice caused a number of people to go ballistic, among them John Beyer who—according to the *New York Post*—went to Joseph Seymour, head of the Port Authority, to grouse about the substitution of the two developer plans for similar schemes his office had done. At this point, Seymour and Lou Thomson—Director of the LMDC—agreed to replace the two developer plans with the Beyer Blinder Belle versions, a move which, in turn, caused a number of the original members of the LMDC task force to become enraged at the high-handed violation of "the process." Arguably, though, the coup executed by Seymour and Thomson can be seen as restoring the process which, in theory, should only have qualified the plans produced by the architects "publicly" designated to do so.

By the end of July, the LMDC—barraged with criticism from all sides and losing its political backing from the mayor and the governor, both of whom were critical of the initial schemes—itself came out in favor of opening the process to smaller firms and to offices from abroad. No procedures have yet been announced and there is no indication of how level the playing field will be for those who wish to be involved. Nevertheless, this is a start. Blather about participation notwithstanding, however, it is clear that architects with millions in public money to spend, and with the guaranteed sanction and public relations efforts of officialdom, are working at something of an advantage: the wherewithal to produce volumes of computerized eye candy and get it immediately into the media distorts the discussion fundamentally because other ideas simply cannot be heard.

Perhaps it is time for a little less management and a little more democracy. Let us immediately have, not a competition, but an open call for ideas from around the world. Let us spend some money on a wonderfully well-presented exhibition. Let us give people some authentic choices instead of an elaborate scheme for pulling the wool over their eyes. Let us have the kind of real discussion that can only come from having real alternatives.

CROSS

THE S

**ALMOST IMMEDIATELY, CONVERSATION ABOUT RECONSTRUCTION TURN-
ED TO THE RESTORATION OF THE GRID OF STREETS THAT HAD BEEN
OBLITERATED BY THE CONSTRUCTION OF THE TRADE CENTER.** The elevated podium on which the towers sat had precluded circultion both
east-west and north-south across the huge site. Debate was couched primarily in terms of such access, of the renewed possibility for easy connections. While restoring such freedom of movement was and is vital,
the foregrounding of the restoration of the street grid was a huge red
herring, presenting the grid as if it were the only way to to move comfortably across the site. What remained unspoken was that the street
grid was not simply a means for crossing the site, but of organizing it:
the re-imposition of the grid would immediately yield a series of dis-
crete parcels, ideal for development but not necessarily yielding the
most coherent — or beautiful — community or space.

ING

TE

The three studies presented here are simply meant to show that there are alternatives to the grid for crossing the site. The most obvious —and most conceptually convenient—is, of course, simply to leave the site as a single open space, crossable in any direction. Another possibility is a skewed grid, organized around the ends of surrounding streets and distorted by the location of the footprints. A final alternative is radial, based on the idea of the convergence of surrounding circulation on a major space at the center of the site.

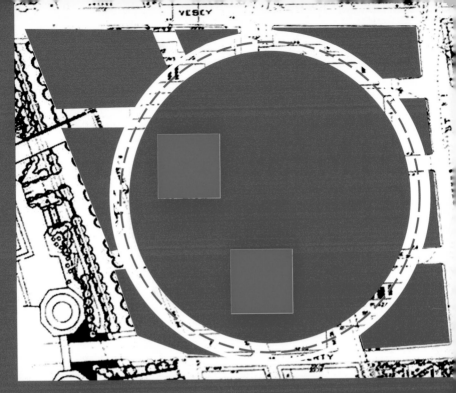

↑ Open Crossing

↖ Skewed Grid
← Radial

THE DIMENSIONS OF AURA

THE CLEARING OF THE SITE WAS ACCOMPANIED BY WIDESPREAD CLAIMS FOR ITS SANCTITY. Everyone recognized that this was sacred ground, a gravesite, a place permanently marked by tragedy. In those first days, many of us called for the preservation of the entire fourteen acres as a memorial to the three thousand victims of the horrendous attack.

In the intervening months, this idea — most forcefully demanded by the survivors of those who died — has quietly disappeared. The media barely refer to it and none of the schemes proposed to date by the Lower Manhattan Development Corporation — all of which call for the restoration of massive amounts of office and retail space — even approach such a solution. Indeed, among those officially empowered to make choices, there seems to be a consensus that such a mode of remembering is either impractical, overly sentimental, or in some other way simply disproportionate.

It is clear that most consider the site permanently saturated with solemnity and therefore entitled to special consideration, some exception from business as usual. Just as the battlefields of the Civil War, the site of the Murrah Federal Building in Oklahoma City, or the African Burial Ground in lower Manhattan have been marked and retain the power to arouse tremendous emotions when encroachment threatens, the World Trade Center site has an aura that must remain unbreached.

The question is, what is its range and weight? What is its influence on both its immediate and extended environments?

As of now, the "footprints" of the towers have come to serve as a metonymic representation of the larger space of this tragic event. Since Governor Pataki's pledge that nothing would be built on these footprints, their preservation as the space of memorialization has become the default memorial site. Indeed, most of the plans promulgated by the LMDC respected the idea of the inviolability of the footprints, despite the inclusion of massive construction around them.

Given the now cleared site, the footprints are, however, an entirely conceptual notion: there is no longer any physical evidence of them. To be sure, the "bathtub"—the vast retaining wall that surrounds the entire site—is legibly clear and has the potential to figure in a memorial. But the footprints themselves would have to be reconstituted in any scheme to "preserve" them. Would it make a difference if they were shifted by a few feet? Does their sanctity demand that nothing intrude in the airspace above them? Does their auratic power extend into the earth below?

A remarkable hair-splitting proposition has just been announced by the Port Authority that offers the first precise measurement of the official dimensions of this aura. Under pressure from survivor groups the PA has concluded that locating commercial space beneath the footprints is inappropriate but that retaining the alignment of the PATH commuter train (presumably a less crass, more public use) under the former south tower is okay, despite survivor arguments that the sacred space extends to bedrock.

This conundrum is deepened by a further displacement. Although much public debate has revolved around the appropriateness of building a "cemetery" on the site, the lack of human remains compromises the usefulness of the model. Equally, the frequently invoked analogy of a battlefield seems inappropriate to the site of a mass murder of civilians. And there is difficulty in establishing agreement about the basic character of the event itself—one constituency calls for a memorial with a widely dispersed aura while another prioritizes the restoration of commercial activity, with some going so far as to demand reconstruction of the twin towers.

The city can't find a way to decide among these claims: the ethical dimensions of this question are well beyond the ken of the businessmen and bureaucrats who dominate the LMDC and Port Authority, bodies empowered to decide on the future of the site. These agencies offer plans in which a "memorial" is treated as mere adjunct to the larger development and not its driver. This distinction is fundamental and must undergird a serious debate that has yet to take place in the corridors of power.

The recent parsing by the Port Authority of the reach of the footprints is useful in locating the aura in both space and use. After all, the question isn't simply how close normal life should be permitted to come but what activities are to be considered respectful. As one bridles at the thought of a casino on Omaha Beach or a McDonald's at Verdun—and just as tremendous protest recently greeted the opening of a disco next to Auschwitz—so it should be clear that some things cannot come too close to Ground Zero, wherever we decide to locate it.

In a real estate economy in which value (and meaning) is measured in inches, the care with which we discuss these questions will have tremendous bearing on the meaning of this place for future generations and on its role in the larger context of the physical pattern of New York City. The question is whether a compromise between contending interests—financial, transportation, memorial, etc.—can yield a vision for the place. The conflict is not simply between a terribly banal, a-little-something-for-everyone, politics and a democratic process in which all voices are heard and weighed to advance a larger idea of the common good. Such matters of a collectively formed memory are the not the subject for compromise but the place for a more spiritual consensus.

Every memorial invents the event it recalls. The event "9/11" cannot simply be absorbed into things as they are: a year later it still exceeds our ability to describe it and it always will. It is only what happens now —what we do about this event and how we mark it—that will define the meaning of the horrific act. Until the endlessly "realistic" language of current discussion can be changed to accommodate this perspective, the victims of this awful crime will not have been served.

THE GENERAL ACCEPTANCE OF THE ICONOGRAPHY OF THE "FOOT-PRINTS" OF THE TOWERS HAS CLEARLY BECOME THE FORMAL TERRAIN ON WHICH A MEMORIAL MUST EXPRESS ITSELF. The fact that no trace of the footprints remains means that they must be reinvented from scratch, that both their measurements and their force must be defined. The project presented here is an assertion of what seems a natural auratic throw for these forms. At a minimum, this would seem to entail everything within the lost perimeter of the towers and extend down to bedrock and up to the heavens. Anything less is clearly a compromise and must be explicitly understood as such.

In this sketch, a simple stair from grade descends 72 feet to the level of bedrock with clear space overhead. The two footprints are joined by a third element—a subterranean memorial hall—in which the names of all the victims are inscribed. Below grade—in the transit hall—the footprints would register as impassable walls. The act of going down stairs, passing through the memorial hall, and climbing up would provide a ritual of participation and recall kinesthetically the means by which many escaped, many were trapped, and many performed their stunning acts of heroism.

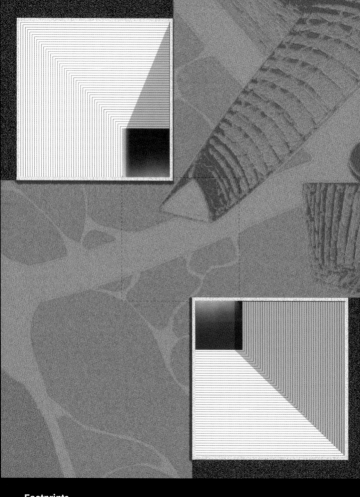

Footprints

Section through The Hall of Names

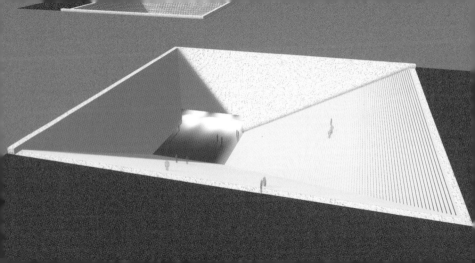

THE W

PEACE

DOME

THE DISCUSSION SIMPLY GOT TO FORM TOO FAST. Perhaps there was no avoiding it, given the pressure. And there was a certain logic to the restoration of the skyline, to patching the gaping hole. Given the growing certainty that building was going to be the "solution," we speculated about a form other than that of a tower or towers. We wanted to resist both the triumphalist phallomorphology of a bigger, higher, "better" version of the Trade Towers and to find a form that spoke to issues of harmony and peace while assuming some prominence on the skyline.

A dome seemed at once legible, evocative, and different. As a place for people to gather at all times of the year, it satisfied what seemed to be the most important activity the site should embrace — peaceable assembly. And, commemoration and marking could take place with the reconstruction of the footprints and the planting of lush, year-round gardens. Site organization sought to allow people to flow across from every adjoining street and the big dome also served as an enclosure for

ORLD

the transit center that would inevitably become part of any project. Finally, we placed a series of crescent-shaped towers within the dome to house other uses we thought important: a panoply of cultural institutions and a home for people and organizations working for world peace, perhaps the UN or a center for NGO's. Although the form of these structures was not strictly predictive of the style of their occupation, it did seem very important to assert that that all uses were not equivalent and that reconstruction of the site had to be predicated on an idea of choosing the appropriate ones.

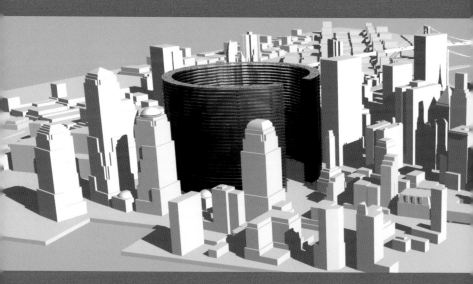

A 55-story extrusion of the protective berm proposed for
the site would reproduce the volume of space lost on 9/11

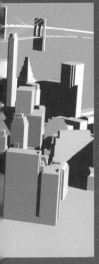

Revealed:
Downtown's

ME OF PEACE

THE WORLD PEACE DOME
SEPTEMBER 2002

North and south views along
a pedestrianized West Street

Aerial view

View south showing Greenwich Street
passing through the dome

HERBERT'S LIST

FINDING A NEW FORM FOR GROUND ZERO DEMANDS THAT TWO DIVER-GENT APPROACHES BE PURSUED SIMULTANEOUSLY. The first is the messy, disputative process of building public consensus about the future meaning and use of the site. From this discussion must come answers about the sacrality of the site — its aura and dimensions — about the mix of program, and about the extent and character of transportation infrastructure. This deliberation must also engage the prospects of reconstruction for neighborhoods beyond the immediate site, indeed, for the city as a whole. The second major process, in contrast, is artistic and visionary. This relies on individual acts of imagination to produce ideas that broaden the range of possibilities before the public and to provide the basis for genuinely informed choice.

The Lower Manhattan Development Corporation has not understood the importance of this relationship. The derision that greeted their first proposals was a response to their seeming indifference to public feelings about the use of the site and to the mediocrity of physical designs put forward. Both of these failures sprang from a deep poverty of imagination and from a remarkably undemocratic desire to control the terms of any discussion. As a result, this conceptual and artistic deficit has been left to be made up by individual creators and by the abundance of unofficial planning alliances that have grown in the wake of the disaster. However, because none of these efforts have any official standing, their audibility to the LMDC is a matter of prestige and connections: the LMDC has opened their inquiry only under pressure.

If there were a forum in which one might have expected to see presented the great variety of suggestions produced in the last year, it is the *New York Times*. Our newspaper of record, however, has been AWOL. Although this indifference obviously flows from the paper's upper echelons, much of the responsibility for the crabbed coverage of possible alternatives is due to the gatekeeping role played by the newspaper's architectural critic, Herbert Muschamp.

Muschamp has been acerbic in his opposition to the corruptions of the LMDC. And, his scathing commentary on the six misbegotten plans released in July was immediately echoed on the editorial page, which, in a leader headlined "The Downtown We Don't Want," characterized the schemes as "dreary (and) leaden" and argued that no plan with that amount of commercial space would fly. It also suggested — following on a proposal made by the LMDC and others — "how much better residential and commercial areas would cohere if West Street can be submerged and covered with a promenade or a park."

The very next day, though, Muschamp weighed in with a short "appraisal" in which he lavished praise on quite a different vision. Plucking one of the site diagrams published in the run-up to the LMDC 6 by New York/New Visions in their exemplary analytical document, Muschamp trumpeted the discovery of a scheme of "remarkable elegance" and "unmatched conceptual beauty." This turned out to be a *parti* in which the buried West Street was topped not with a "promenade or park" but by a series of developable blocks. Authorship of the plan was attributed to the architect Frederic Schwarz who had been busily working officialdom on its behalf, now detached from the larger project of New York/New Visions from which it had emerged.

While most of the July LMDC schemes had proposed to bury West Street, the Schwarz plan differed in suggesting that buildings be constructed atop the tunnel. The idea is not unfamiliar: Schwarz cut his architectural teeth in the Venturi, Scott-Brown office working on Westway, and this scheme revisits the basic idea behind that project:

the use of publicly funded infrastructure to create sites for private speculation. Muschamp suggests this as a logical way to alleviate pressure
on the Trade Center Site because it offers an alternative territory for
development, though neither Muschamp nor Schwarz has advanced any
argument for the formal superiority of such a development to the creation of additional green and public space atop the buried roadway.

Muschamp presents this plan as if it were the only solution to the
question of off-site replacement space. Ignored are millions of square
feet currently vacant and the numerous unbuilt and underbuilt sites
downtown (together more than enough to replace the Trade Center
twice over), as well as the possibility of replacing lost space elsewhere in
the city. Although contemptuous of developer demands for immediate
replacement of lost income streams , ("the lease made me do it" he acid-
ly began one of his pieces), his plan accomplishes just that, predicated
on the ultimate in developer reasoning: the logic of the parcel.

Such parcels, however, were also the ground for an exercise in
Muschamp's central critical operation: compiling a list of his favorite
architects. Having prepared the ground by suggesting that the parcel-
lized development of West Street was the only logical way forward,
Muschamp—playing Napoleon III to Schwarz's Haussman—selected a
group to implement the plan, and their risible efforts were published
with great fanfare in the New York Times Magazine in early September.
While there were a few tasty images among the proposals, the schemes
were largely undercooked, with no urbanistic glue to give spatial
and circulatory logic to their ensemble. Indeed, Muschamp's branding
approach made Larry Silverstein look like Cosimo di Medici.

Muschamp's plan also suggests that the Twin Towers *themselves* be
rebuilt—slightly southeast of the original site! But wasn't the "remarkable elegance" of the Schwarz plan supposedly in obviating the need to
replace the towers? To be sure, the buildings shown are Trade Towers
with a twist: the huge structures have been torqued, according to
Muschamp, to resemble "a pair of candlesticks of unidentified authorship." In fact they resemble fairly precisely a widely disseminat-
ed scheme by Richard Dattner, whose authorship is submerged in the
claim that these buildings "enjoy a variety of sources." I am reminded
of the undergraduate strategy of over-supplying footnotes to conceal

a plagarised source.

The editors at the *Times*—despite their earlier position in favor of a park—immediately started rolling this log. The week following publication of Muschamp's plan, a piece appeared in the "Home" section entitled "At Home With Frederic Schwarz, The Man Who Dared the City to Think Again." After congratulating him once more for his "aspirational" scheme, the writer described Schwarz's Soho loft, his girlfriend, and his breakfast. The shelter section of the Times is obsessed with pedigree. Likewise, Herbert's lists are always about the celebrity, and Schwarz had to be turned into one so the provenance of a widely bruited suggestion could be attributed to him.

This celebrity "authority" received a further spin in the publication by *New York Magazine* of its own collection of schemes in a September 11 special issue, organized by its architecture critic, Joseph Giovannini. Site-wide designs were sought from six architects with results that certainly raised more interesting urbanistic issues than Muschamp's (not so) exquisite corpse, while still feeding the celebrity beast. Indeed, two of Giovannini's six designers were also on Herbert's list! For *New York*, Peter Eisenman and Zaha Hadid produced completely different, more fully elaborated, schemes.

Stung by the attacks on its own six schemes, the LMDC had announced in August that it wanted its own hip list and was prepared to pony up a puny sum to sponsor a further six schemes. And whom did the LMDC choose from the 400 who applied (full disclosure: me among them)? THE SAME PEOPLE! Frederic Schwarz (already backpedalling away from the idea of burying West Street in face of rising community opposition), David Rockwell, and Rafael Vinoly—all from Herb's list—dominate one team. Another is comprised of Masters-of-the-Universe, Steven Holl, Charles Gwathmey, Richard Meier and trifecta winner Peter Eisenman—Herbert's list, one and all. Norman Foster, architect for the headquarters of Swiss RE, Silverstein's insurer, makes the cut as does Danniel Liebeskind, our leading iconographer of trauma. There is an interesting, if jerry-rigged, team made up of a group of younger stars from the US and Europe. And, appallingly, the final slot goes to Skidmore, Owings, and Merrill, making this the fourth such commission they've received. They are designing Number Seven for

Larry Silverstein. They've done a site-wide scheme for Larry Silverstein (featuring a very tall tower!). They've done a planning study for the east side of downtown for Carl Weisbrod (head of the downtown BID and member of the LMDC board). Why not just hand them the commission now?

Immediately following the LMDC selection of his list, Muschamp returned the favor, doing a full 180, writing that the LMDC, former masters of malevolence and implacable foes of art, now is likely to "change the course of cultural life in New York." Come again? What would really change the course of cultural (and political) life in New York would be an open process, a genuine competition, in which public bodies (not to mention architectural critics) devoted themselves to promoting the widest — and wildest — styles of inclusion, not this endless, mad, cronyism. And, am I wrong to think that in offering his own proposal at this stage of the game, Muschamp has stepped over the critical line, compromising his future ability to judge developments dispassionately?

THE

LOTUS

**AS WE CONTINUED TO LOOK AT POSSIBILITIES FOR BUILDING ON THE
SITE, WE BECAME MORE INTRIGUED WITH THE FORMAL POSSIBILITIES
OF THE TOWERS DESIGNED FOR THE INTERIOR OF THE WORLD PEACE
DOME.** Our next move was to remove the huge enclosure and let the ten-
drils grow and loosen formally, unconstrained by the formerly spherical
condition but still informed by it. The metaphor of a flower unfolding
hovered over the project as we worked through this second iteration.
Initial drawings show the buildings as a kind of Fata Morgana, unat-
tached wisps mingling with more rooted structures. Looking back, there
seems to be something both floral and flame-like in these forms. This
reflects both memory and ambivalence. More important, the paring
away of the dome and the ephemerality of the sketches recall my earli-
est feelings about the future of the site, that it should be left alone for
a long time before any decision was taken about reconstruction.

Nevertheless, we pressed on to test the architectural viability of the scheme. The site organization worked well enough and the towers were viable. There was plenty of room for the inclusion of cultural institutions below grade and within the wide bases of the towers. Taking note of a private development proposal for a tower on the site of the proposed MTA transportation center on Broadway, we designed a covered galleria over Dey Street as a grand transport concourse, connecting the collection of lines converging beneath Ground Zero with those concentrated further east. The plan also includes the rebuilding of the block to the south of Dey Street and the inclusion of a major cultural space — perhaps the City Opera — within it.

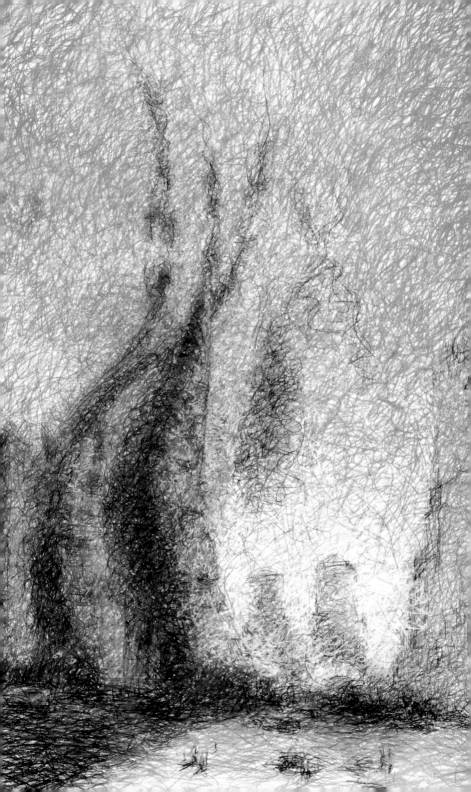

Twin towers as double helix

Section through Dey Street looking north

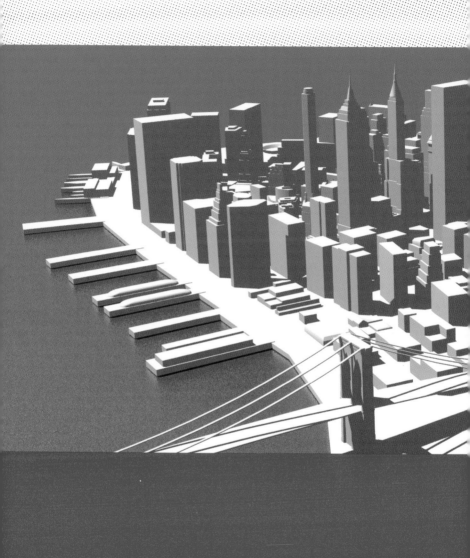

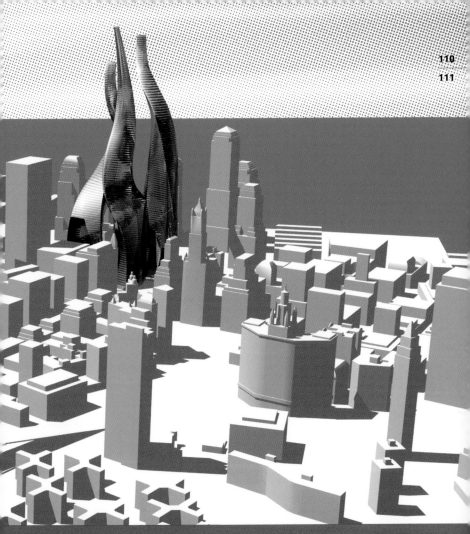

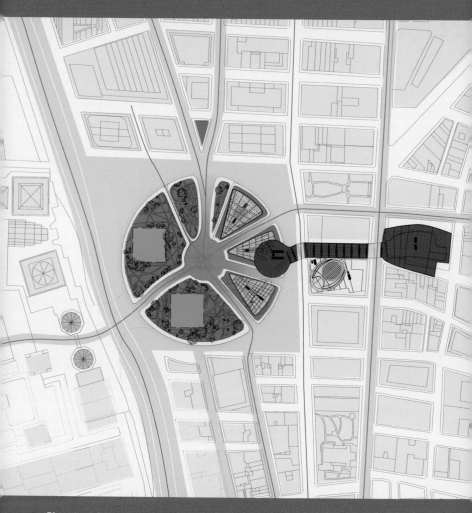

Plan at grade

0   200'

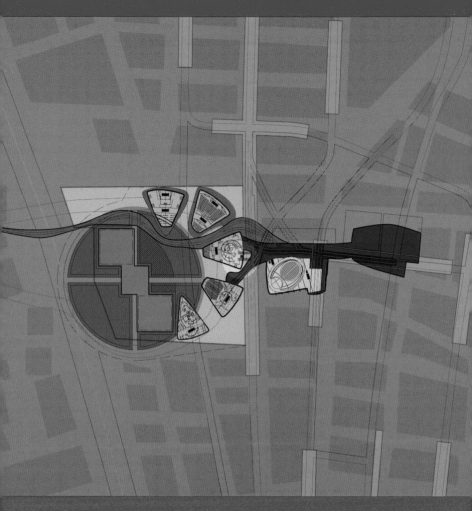

Plan at lower concourse level

SECURITY

**A RECENT AD FOR A "HOMELAND SECURITY SUMMIT AND EXPOSITION"
BORE THE HEADLINE, "GRAB CENTER STAGE IN A $138 BILLION MARKET."**
Clearly paranoia is a growth industry, and the proliferation of conferences and meetings to discuss its implications is staggering. Since September 11, the nation has been consumed with its "war on terror," and the lens of fear increasingly diffracts the meaning of everyday life. From the bomb detectors at the airport to the rise in ethnic profiling, to the visa difficulties of the students we admit from abroad, to the Pentagon's sinister data-mining project under the supervision of Admiral John Poindexter of Iran-Contra fame, to new tics in our private behaviors, the culture is suffused with incitements to anxiety as the media fixates on the imminence of terror.

My own private internalization of this fear strikes me from time to time on my walk home from my studio, which takes me past a large federal building that houses, among other offices, the passport agency. As I approach this block, I often find myself thinking about car bombs. After particularly anxious days at work, I sometimes imagine I have spotted the lethal vehicle (generally some nondescript mini-van) set to explode. I have walked blocks out of my way to circumnavigate the building and the impending fatal blast.

We measure the environment in the light of our perception of its perils. Whether skirting dark streets at night, mapping and avoiding "dangerous" neighborhoods, or staying out of tall buildings, the human geography of the city entails assessments of convenience, pleasure, and risks. Our problem nowadays is that we are creating an urbanism predicated primarily on risk avoidance, one likely, in its more extreme versions, to have a terrible effect on fundamental ideas of the good city. To the degree that we acquiesce, we become complicit in a cycle of exacerbated paranoia, in creating a bunker mentality.

There are both material and immaterial bunkers. The material variety — already abundant — includes the proliferation of biometric checkpoints, credentials checks, hardened construction, defensive bollards, ditches around "high-value" targets, and so on. The immaterial fortifications are more internal, and revolve around modifications to our own behavior: anxiety about setting out, willingness to permit prying into our private information, suspicion of people who somehow look "wrong," or demands for accelerated police action. Internalizing the means of our own repression, we risk allowing fanatics to turn us into totalitarians.

In his book, *The Birth of the Clinic*, Michel Foucault describes the response of a town in the Middle Ages to an outbreak of plague. Lacking modern medical knowledge, the town — on a signal from the authorities — adopted a state of hyper-orderliness, making personal movements geometrical and activities clock-work. This imposition of an apparently rational style of urban behavior was meant as an antidote to the evil and irrationality of the disease. Needless to say, it was not effective, although — in a typically *post hoc propter hoc* argument — the eventual waning of the plague could be attributed to the only course of action actually taken.

And this will be our delusion too if we acquiesce in the re-imagination of our cities as battlegrounds, rushing to superimpose military order in a place that requires very different styles of discipline, hierarchy, and choice. We have all suffered the new inconveniences of the main focus of current security efforts: the air transport corridor. The time on line waiting to pass through detectors, the force of interrogators asking us whether someone has given us something to carry on the plane, the large numbers of armed personnel, the endless thresholds at which we are scanned and our progress through space mapped step-by-step, have all become part of the background of our lives. Making this process convenient by making it invisible is not one in which we should participate uncritically. We may want to glide from the concourse to the gate, but I, for one, want to know when I am being electronically patted down and to whom this information is being conveyed.

Given the genuine risks that we do face, however, the question becomes whether there is any meeting ground between the need for precautions and the on-going project of urban amelioration — the construction of cities that are humane, democratic, and sustainable. There are several potential points of convergence between these concerns, places where energy might be focused to make our cities both more comfortably secure and more comfortably free, a kind of "peace dividend" from a number of the measures we are likely to take based strictly on questions of security.

We can begin by extracting questions of safety and security from a narrow focus on terror. So many more of us die falling down stairs or in automobile accidents than in wars or terror attacks that a little perspective is necessary, a realistic sense of proportion about the sites and organization of investment: the risk of being struck down crossing the street by an suv is far higher than the worst bin Laden can do. I don't mean to be glib, but it is important to understand that the fear mongering of the moment is based on a set of fundamentally political agendas. How then to de-politicize the idea of safety, or rather, how to democratize it?

To state the obvious, the project of making cities and buildings safer must encompass needed improvements for security from other risks. Clearly, reinforcing buildings against seismic hazards also brings greater safety from other externally induced structural traumas. Even more important is the dramatic improvement of fire safety. Many of the lives lost in the Trade Center disaster might have been saved with better fire abatement systems, with increased means of egress, with better internal communication, with careful attention to the presence of toxic and other flammable materials. These are steps that need to be taken on an urgent basis, especially in tall buildings.

If September 11 can serve as a goad for us to address the threats mounted to buildings, this is to the good. However, even here we risk a kind of parochialization of risk. Building safety must also encompass the effects of architecture on climate, the health-related effects of "sick building syndrome," the damage to workers and resources in remote locations, the flat-out toxicity of many of the materials with which we build, the dangers of the building process, and the insecurities engendered by the massive consumption of energy by buildings (itself one of the reasons for the current rush to war). A national policy based on securing the means for continuing the cycle of hyper-consumption has enormous and unfaced planetary and political consequences. Building security goes way beyond metal detectors and security guards.

One of the striking scenes in New York following September 11 was a dramatic rearrangement in the movement of traffic in the city, when access to Manhattan via bridges and tunnels was limited. Emergency vehicles were able to flow without impediment. Streets were pretenaturally quiet. Pedestrians were predominant. Car-pooling was enforced.

In the process of rethinking the city after 9/11, the management of systems of movement is perhaps the central opportunity for synergy between security and urbanity. In New York, we have the opportunity for a dramatic pedestrianization downtown, with Ground Zero as its center. This local greening might be accompanied by a large-scale reduction in private vehicles in the city as a whole and the replacement of no-longer-required road space with parks, bikeways, and other public amenities. The moment is also ripe for a more rational system of goods distribution and delivery, one that utilizes both our subways and waterways. Both security and urbanity would benefit from more rigorous management of city traffic: greater efficiency in delivering milk might have an ancillary benefit in greater inefficiency in delivering bombs.

A general increase in architectural and urban "inefficiency" could, indeed, have many positive effects. A multiplication of routes, and mixing of scales would humanize cities too straightforward and homogeneous. Structural over-design and redundancy could increase both safety and complexity. An architecture more integrated with the earth around it would enhance thermal performance, environmental continuity and variety of use. The sort of bottom-line "inefficiency" represented by European-style regulations limiting the dimensions of office floor plates to guarantee inhabitants access to light and air would create buildings that are psychically and physically both safer and friendlier.

As Jane Jacobs has observed, strong neighborhoods are safe neighborhoods. Her theory suggested local spatial supervision based not on centralized means of surveillance but on the extension of the idea of neighborliness. Although anonymity is a prized value in city life, it is one among many, and there are styles of intrusion that are more and less civic. The grandmother leaning out of the window keeping an eye on the street is a radically different solution than M-16-toting guardsmen manning checkpoints downtown. It is not liberal sentimentality to suggest that building strong neighborhoods, neighborhoods with complex nets of relationship and interdependency, is an intrinsically superior style of security than CCTV on every corner. Our personal participation in the security of our cities and neighborhoods should grow from a sense of decorum, not fear.

By extension, we are now presented with an opportunity to rethink the nature of business and commercial concentrations within individ-

ual cites. The same technologies that allow corporate headquarters and call centers to grow on green-field sites far from the pleasures and conveniences of town can also allow us to adopt a policy of local decentralization based not simply on security from terror but on the convenience of building sustainable communities in which living, working, education, culture, recreation—all the components of the good urban life—can be planned comprehensively: metropolitanization rather than global dispersion. In terms of the real economic development of New York City, for example, it would seem far more productive to apply the massive capital that is about to be squandered on unneeded offices downtown to the reconstruction of the Bronx Hub or 125th Street.

The key to our security is neither the construction of new fortifications nor a willingness to progressively surrender our shrinking rights of privacy to the tender mercies of the national security state. Our best defense against terror lies in the strength of our democratic institutions and of our human character: armament is not a substitute for a culture of compassion and generosity. The horrible events of 9/11 are not a call to arms but to increase the peace.

A BRIEF FOR RE— CONSTRUCTION

1   People must be free to gather. Uncoerced assembly is democracy
    expressed in space.

2   A wide range of rites and rituals of remembrance must be accomodated.

3   The need of survivors of the tragedy to gather must be served.

4   The site must be understood as a single whole.

5   The site must be easily entered and crossed. All existing streets
    and major building entrances surrounding the site should provide
    direct pedestrian access to it.

6   The literal continuation of streets and sidewalks is only the most
    obvious strategy.

7   The primary datum for crossing must be the grade of the site.

8   That grade should align with surrounding contours.

9   The event must be measured and marked.

10 This must include the footprints of the towers and their ramification
    in three dimensions, extending to bedrock and the heavens.

11 These ramifications shall engage both space and use.

12 The site must permanently educate about the nature of the events
that happened there.

13 The site should be a point of focus for a well mixed urbanity downtown.

14 Any construction at the large scale must not preclude the possibility
of the small.

15 The site should serve as a point of growth and spreading of green space.

16 The site should be well connected to its neighborhood, to New York City,
and to the world.

17 The transportation infrastructure already below and near the site
is crucial to these connections.

18 Many people should live near the site.

19 The elaboration of the site should support existing social, economic,
and natural ecologies.

20 The site should be exceptional.

WHO DECIDES?

**IN A PHRASE THAT CAN CHARITABLY ONLY BE DESCRIBED AS DISINGEN-
UOUS, LOU THOMSON, PRESIDENT OF THE LMDC, ANNOUNCED THAT THE
SEVEN NEW PROPOSALS FOR THE WORLD TRADE CENTER SITE "WERE
FORGED IN A DEMOCRATIC PROCESS."** If only it were so: deliberations
over the future of Ground Zero have become progressively less and less
democratic as layer after layer of bureaucracy is inserted between the
citizens of New York and the final decision about the site. The situa-
tion was bad to begin with, with the most powerful players the Port
Authority, an agency of Olympian detachment from public control, and
its largest lessor, Larry Silverstein, whose venal values were nowhere
more clearly revealed than in his attempt to persuade his insurers,
Swiss RE, that two catastrophes had occurred on the site and that his
payout should, therefore, be double.

In late 2001, another player, the LMDC — appointed by Governor
Pataki and Mayor Giuliani — entered the picture and quickly hired an
"outside" planner (chosen by opaque criteria from a list confined to a
small number of giant corporate architectural firms) who (along with
another firm, chosen behind closed doors by the LMDC) prepared the
misbegotten, conceptually identical, and universally derided office
schemes presented in July. Almost immediately, the clearly embarrassed
LMDC announced that in order to elicit more "visionary" architectural

proposals, they would conduct what has widely been misrepresented as a "competition." This again involved the appointment of a "non-political" committee by the LMDC to choose six new teams which nevertheless managed to include the architects already working for Larry Silverstein, the architect of the Swiss RE headquarters, a group of architects heavily promoted by the *New York Times*, and the architects already introduced via the back door by the LMDC for the first go-round.

Although the seven new schemes offer some dramatic form-making, they actually serve to make the process even more obscure and inaccessible by the sheer multiplication of hidden interests and vague procedures. Although the idea of more alternatives is crucial to a wise and democratic decision about the future of Ground Zero, the powers in charge are using the additional choices to cover a fundamental narrowing of options. It isn't simply that there will be neither adjudication among — nor obligation to — any idea broached by the "competitors," but that virtually every scheme submitted serves to legitimate an even more primary lack of choice: that of the program for the site. While several of the projects include interesting ideas for the memorial, they are — like their roundly reviled predecessors — predominantly strategies for locating vast amounts of office space on or near the site, including various versions of the world's tallest building.

Two fundamentally bogus arguments are offered as proof of the democratic character of this process. The first is that the LMDC and the Port Authority, and Larry Silverstein, have all "listened" to what people have had to say. This is a familiar dodge of autocrats everywhere, reminiscent of those audiences held by Saudi Arabian princes — often advertised as their own culturally special form of democratic governance — in which boons are selectively offered to long lines of mendicants. Yet democracy is not simply a matter of being heard but of having the power to sway the course of events, and no amount of focus groups or sessions of "Listening to the People" offer that rightful certainty of power.

The second style of democracy is more indigenous to the way New York itself plans and it lies in the "power" of individuals (or Community Boards, or civic groups) to just say no, whether through foot-dragging, litigation, demonstrations, or civil disobedience. Such a democracy by negation can help curb the excesses of both elected and unelected officials but it is, at best, a gamble: no statute obliges anyone to pay attention, and initiative belongs to the powerful. Indeed, the mess we are in grows precisely out of the extra-legal, back-room, style of planning that has dominated the reconstruction process from the outset, a reflection of the contemporary grail of efficient development as building "as of right," which is to say, without any public input.

Although planning, architecture, and democracy are difficult bedfellows — no amount of public participation can substitute for either artistic genius or genuine expertise — rebuilding Ground Zero is too important to the collective life and identity of New York to be relegated to the bottom-line, business-as-usual mentality that is driving it. What is excluded (in much the same way survivor representatives were excluded from the board of the LMDC) is the idea that the plan must be driven by the memorial, the idea that commercial activity is not the invariable default, the idea that designs might come from people other than those carefully filtered by the uninspiring leadership of the LMDC or produced in secrecy by the Port Authority or the lessor.

American democracy is not direct but representative. Such representation is least responsive when it is most attenuated, when decision makers are farthest removed from popular recall. Downtown, decisions are being made by the appointees of the appointees of the appointees of elected officials. But perhaps it is time for a simpler strategy: let the people decide themselves. I don't mean to suggest this as a universal formula for planning. As a general matter, direct democracy is a terrible way to plan, a lowest common denominator approach. But this is a special case. It is important to recognize that September 11 was an event; that is, it happened to all of us, not to buildings or businesses or an area downtown. September 11 included everyone, and it is the extraordinariness of this fact that must be acknowledged by what gets done at Ground Zero. The process of deciding becomes, in this instance, far more important than the efficiency, profitability, or even the aesthetics of whatever is finally built.

The first step remains to find a way to ask the public about its desires for the use of Ground Zero that begins with *all* options on the table. The duty of a democratic politics includes the education of its citizenship, the provision of the necessary information for informed debate. The crowds that now gather in the Winter Garden to look at the new schemes testify both to the strength of feeling and the depth of interest in the future of the site and to the public's ability to assimilate architectural and planning ideas. But why just these seven choices? Why must the LMDC be interposed as gatekeeper, narrowing and coercing possibilities instead of helping to give us a look at every idea that might (or might not) work on the site? Why can't we have an open invitation to anyone with a cogently drawn plan or intelligibly written text to post it at the Javits Center or the Winter Garden for a month or two in order to fully draw out the conversation about possibilities?

This profusion of ideas (and there are thousands out there) would allow the public to coalesce around a program, to make known what they want built on this fraught site. An open process would also allow the public to make fiscal decisions properly its own, to decide how to pay for the memorial, how to compensate stakeholders, if necessary, and what transit infrastructure improvements to include. Then, and only then, can there be a genuine competition for the entire site. Such a competition would seek solutions that merge memory and moving on and must be open to all. And, would it be completely unreasonable for the public to choose the winner? Indeed, the only collectivity that has shown any wisdom in this corrupt and depressing process has been the public in its decisive rejection of the mediocre work of our mediocre public servants and private entrepreneurs.

The answer to terror is neither muscle flexing nor the oblivious politburo-style of the LMDC and the Port Authority, as well as their spurious and short-sighted "practicalities." The real reply is an excess of democracy, flamboyant participation. Although it's more than improbable (and happily so) that the public—especially with the experience of tragedy so near—will agree unanimously on a solution, the conversation is guaranteed to yield a more forceful and inventive solution than anything we have seen thus far. The process of arriving at the decision would be its own memorial.

AND
THEN
THERE
WERE TWO

THE "COMPETITION" FOR THE DESIGN OF GROUND ZERO HAS NOW ARRIVED AT TWO FINALISTS, DANIEL LIEBESKIND AND THE "THINK" GROUP, SURVIVORS OF A GROUP OF SEVEN HASTILY ASSEMBLED BY THE LMDC TO COVER ITS BELEAGUERED BACKSIDE AFTER AN EMBARRASSINGLY LIMP FIRST EFFORT TO PROVIDE "CHOICES" FOR THE RECONSTRUCTION OF THE SITE. Universally derided for its imaginative poverty and its failure to suggest any use save the restoration of massive commercial activity, the LMDC quickly moved to camouflage its own tiny vision with glossy form.

The gambit of foregrounding Architecture seems to have had the desired effect: questions of alternative uses for the site have been buried under piles of building. Design is offered as a sufficient source of difference—of alternatives—in determining the future of the site with ineffable artistic categories displacing larger questions of program and propriety. And, by concealing its own criteria for selecting the architects for either the first or second round of designs—save the "trust us" gambit of authoritarians everywhere—the remorseless claim that that this was a competition would give the process an artificial flavor of democracy.

Ironically, this has had the effect of pulling the rug out from the one actual competition—for a memorial—the LMDC has long claimed to be organizing. Indeed, so strong is this aspect of each of the two finalists, any project for further memorialization will be desperately constrained. In the Think proposal, the footprints are to be enclosed in the III story cages of their twin "cultural" Eiffel Towers. In the Liebeskind design, the terrain of memorial is below ground and any fresh intervention must figure itself against the huge slurry/wailing wall to be left exposed as the sole architectural survivor of the attack.

A depressing number of people and institutions have risen to the bait, forgetful of earlier calls for an open process in which the memorial—and not the needs of Larry Silverstein or the Port Authority—would be the driver. Of particular interest has been the coverage in *The New York Times*, which has accepted the premise of the "competition" without a disapproving word, focusing, with more than a whiff of collusion, on a narrowly aesthetic reading of the two finalist schemes and on publicity for their progenitors. In a remarkable piece of group-think, this has produced a united front at the *Times* that spans the sections of the paper.

On January 21, the paper editorialized in favor of the Liebeskind project, urging that "one of the two design finalists should certainly be Daniel Liebeskind's soaring garden tower and ground-level memorial that uses the slurry wall holding back the Hudson River as a backdrop. Neither should hark to the past to recreate the twin office towers." The editorial did not suggest which other scheme might be included in the finals, but, as none of the plans proposed recreating the original Twin Towers, one might assume that any plan that suggested twin towers—Norman Foster's, Peterson-Littenberg's, Think's—was being ruled out. The editorial concluded by calling for an architectural and infrastructural plan to be finalized before the competition for the particulars of any memorial take place.

On January 28, Herbert Muschamp, the paper's architecture critic, weighed in with his choice for the winner: the Think group. He touted their twin lattice-work towers as "a work of genius, a towering affirmation of humanism in modern times." Although the humanism of placing windowless cultural facilities eighty stories in the air is surely debatable, Muschamp's choice was unsurprising. Members of the Think team had been the heart of his own attempt to design the site (published in the *Times Magazine* last summer), and he had later touted the brilliance of the idea—per a suggestion of one of the Thinkers—of placing new construction above a buried West Street, leaving Ground Zero free for future deliberation.

The Think solution that was officially submitted to the LMDC abandoned this idea entirely in favor of a plan not unlike those in the first group of shemes for the site so massively derided last summer. Still, they seemed to have had some anxiety over the about-face: in Think's signature renderings of the soaring lattice, the 8 million square feet of proposed office space—lurking round the back of the site—seems to have been coated in stealth materials, invisible to the eye.

On February 4, the two finalists were revealed, and they were the *Times'* two favorites. The paper's earlier elevated tone of ecumenism and support, however, soon disappeared as battle lines between partisans of the two schemes were drawn. On February 6, Muschamp pilloried the Liebeskind project as a "war memorial to a conflict that has scarcely begun" and saddled it with the the worst descriptors in the progressive critic's lexicon: "retro," "nostalgic," "pre-Enlightenment," "premodern," "medieval"..."religious." In contrast, he called the Think project "a soaring affirmation of American values." While Liebeskind is certainly no slouch in the public piety department (indeed, he is a virtual self-igniting Yahrzeit candle, to paraphrase Martin Filler), Muschamp's criticism was totally over the top.

Muschamp claims that memorial architecture has come to stand in the sacred space evacuated by religion—an apotheosis of secular solemnity. In his formulation of the historic separation of civil and religious spheres, he argues that under the "medieval" ideological regime, religion was exploited for political gain, whereas, in our day, political actions are accountable to reason. Left out of this argument is the idea that political actions in democratic culture are also accountable to the desires of citizens. Muschamp and the LMDC see eye to eye in their preference for philosopher kings ("poets are the legislators of the world" he noted in an earlier column) and each sees the problem of Ground Zero as primarily representational, as if the content of the project were purely wrapped up in issues of imagery--an amazingly medieval conceit. The competition is reduced to a matter of iconography: thus, a giant Trade

Center-shaped lattice is intrinsically more modern, progressive, and meaningful than a hole in the ground. Clearly, these are tangled, difficult choices only to be unraveled by clerics like Muschamp.

To bolster this familiar Muschampian reduction of content to pure form, a fashion obligato has been played and replayed in the ancillary sections of the *Times*, reinforcing the idea that what is happening on Ground Zero is simply a contest of styles. In a story in the Sunday Styles section on January 26, Daniel Liebeskind—a lifelong nebbish with a freshly acquired eye for fashion—was celebrated for the fascinating sartorial decision to wear cowboy boots. Accepting at face value his physionomic account of the colossal benefits to his stride and demeanor, the "story" charitably neglected the real reason shortish people often take to stacked heels. The piece also reported admiringly on Liebeskind's Alain Mikli eyeglasses, and in fact was followed a few days later by another story about the eyewear of all the visually challenged finalists—Ken Smith of Think in his Corb redux specs; Fred Schwartz in his horn-rims; Rafael Vinoly in this signature two-pairs-at-once look; and those Miklis again, described by a commentator as "out of control." Whom the *Times* would employ, it first makes *bad*.

As a decision nears, the *Times* has pumped up the volume both in corroboration of the cynical process and in handicapping the winner. A news story the week before the decision was to be made indicated that the political powers that be were tending to the Liebeskind scheme. On the Sunday preceding the decision, a guest column by art historian Marvin Trachtenberg—appearing in the architecture slot generally occupied by Muschamp—denounced the Think scheme as "mainstream modernism," an architecture he associated with "the repression of history, memory, place and identity; the exaltation of functionalism, technology, and the machine," and a "hatred of the city." These scary attributes were alleged to be the spirit behind Think's thing, its "flayed skeletons of the World Trade Center," a description Liebeskind himself used repeatedly in public to describe his competition. As if that weren't enough, Trachtenberg identified what Muschamp had called "a soaring tribute to American values" with "a model taken from the realm of totalitarianism, the famous Monument to the Third Communist International" proposed in 1920 by the great constructivist Vladimir Tatlin.

Liebeskind's design, on the other hand, was lauded for its putative lack of abstraction, its "deeply creative, organic relationship to the specificity of ground zero and its environment and meaning, as well as its accomodation of human needs and sensibilities ... profoundly 'user friendly' on all levels." In short, it was "a miracle of creativity, intelligence, skill, and cutting-edge architectural thought; it looks to the future of architecture, just as Think remains mired in the past.... it reminds us what it means to be human in a city." Say what?

Trachtenberg and Muschamp, looking at schemes alleged to be polar opposites, manage to adduce exactly the same meanings for their favorites. This pathetic argumentation does nothing to advance the contest of ideas and reveals—in its glib and unanalytical associationism (Think is fascist! Liebeskind is humanist! Think is humanist! Liebeskind is fascist!)—just how bankrupt, how feckless, criticism divorced from actual reasoning can be.

The day before the winner was to be announced, the *Times* took three final shots. Under the headline "Designers' Dreams Tempered By Reality," Muschamp described modifications in the finalists' schemes to meet objections from the Port Authority and the LMDC. After some boilerplate about the process having interested the public in architecture, he took a wistful dig at Liebeskind, claiming that because of his particular compromise (shrinking the pit), "the design's symbolic heart no longer exists." While later allowing that Think's scheme had also been shrunk (by the removal of most of the program from within the lattice), he insisted that "the conceptual heart of this design remains intact." Lub dub.

On the same page—under pictures of the finalists surrounded by microphone wielding media types—another article, "Turning A Competition Into A Public Campaign," appeared. This described the twin media blitzes launched by the finalists, ranging from a full court hustle of media outlets, to the hiring of two flacks (one of whom resigned over being second-guessed) by the Liebeskind camp (which had demanded air time with Larry King, Connie Chung, and 60 Minutes), to the hot pursuit of survivor support by both teams. Indeed, the *Times* even reported on its own reporting, citing—not unsardonically—the boots and glasses stories the paper had run.

Finally, a news story reported that the site planning committee of the LMDC had come out in favor of the Think scheme while, as reported earlier, both the Mayor and Governor were supporting Liebeskind. The decision was held to be the result of strong lobbying for Think by Roland Betts, a local business tycoon, best buddy of George Bush and a member of the LMDC Steering Committee, itself charged with the final decision. That committee, however, is dominated by members who owe their jobs to the Governor and the Mayor — Port Authority officials and members of the two administrations. If I were a betting person, I would have to say it looks like Liebeskind.

Either way, though, the *Times* will have called it. Having supported both projects and having piously editorialized about the fairness of the process, the paper has signaled its readiness to fall into line. The more cynical among us are inclined to see the competition as so much smoke-blowing, the real plan awaiting the culmination of multiple deals involving Larry Silverstein, the philistine lease holder; the Port Authority, the site's owner, currently preparing its own plan in secret; the City of New York, still trying to engineer a swap of Ground Zero for the land under JFK and LaGuardia airports; and the Governor, the player with the most cards. Indeed, the only dissent fom all of this has come from Rudy Giuliani, who declared that none of the plans had captured the significance of the event or the place.

Business as usual, as usual.

IN THE END THE VOID

THE DAILY NEWS COULD NOT HAVE BEEN MORE SUCCINCT. Over an image of the plexiglass model of the Liebeskind scheme, the headline, "The new WTC ... Plan Picked, But Reborn Towers Won't Really Look Like This." On Charlie Rose the next evening, the amazingly slimy Larry Silverstein offered his support for "Dan's" plan but allowed that he didn't know that much about skyscrapers. Not a problem his own architects—Skidmore, Owings, and Merrill—wouldn't be able to take care of, though. A telling remark. Many were surprised when—in mid-"competition"—SOM withdrew its own entry which was being hon-choed by Roger Duffy, representing both the un-Childs and the un-Taylor, the two Skidmore partners already working directly for Silverstein.

The strategic withdrawal of SOM is presumably the prelude to their return as the architects for the developer. This widely appreciated like-lihood, has been the source of much consternation focused on the possi-ble loss of the integrity of the Liebeskind proposal. Some of this criticism will surely be forestalled by the recent naming of Liebeskind as "master design architect" for the site, a status to be recognized in contracts from both the Port Authority and the LMDC. According to news reports, this mastery is to extend over the "height, square footage, building outlines, and floor sizes" (presumably including the Viagraic 1776 foot "world's tallest" building of the original proposal), commercial construction, leadership of the design team for the transportation ter-minal and its concourses, and supervision of the development of the memorial to the attack's victims. This likely will include the design of a number of public spaces—including the "wedge of light," the sunken "memorial garden," and a museum devoted to the event.

A tattoo of self-congratulation has been ceaselessly drummed since the LMDC decision, and Liebeskind has been lionized endlessly. The sig-nature glasses and ubiquitous, giddy, grin, the American flag pin that has sprouted in his well-tailored lapel, the black suits and clerical shirts, all have conflated to create the image of the happy mourner. This fits perfectly with the structured ambivalence of the endgame of the process, the solemnity of the development ever receding as the joyous work of building big and restoring cash flow is undertaken. Liebeskind —with his anti-corporate styling—is the perfect foil for the ruling agenda of big business that now dominates. Indeed, the most succinct summation of this portrait of the artist of capital appears in the current issue of a local lower Manhattan paper which holds an image of the grinning Liebeskind, surrounded by smiling, applauding, brokers, as he clutches the wooden hammer with which he has just struck the opening bell of the stock exchange, like Martha Stewart or Michael Eisner.

An alternative site for the world's tallest building (Jersey City)

BACK ZERO

A CONVERSATION IS BEING CLOSED. A public process—the most important planning project of my lifetime in New York City—has been
hijacked by a small cohort of self-interested mediocrities who have simply reimposed the functional and ideological program that was there
before. The open competition of ideas that should have determined the
future of the site will now never take place. There will be a competition
—under the sanction and supervision of the same people who so deafly
pursued their narrow vision of reconstruction—for a marker to be
placed at the bottom of the thirty foot pit that the "master architect"
will provide. How will this memorial be constrained? Liebeskind, who
showed a complete willingness to compromise his ideas to secure the
job, raised the floor of the excavation forty feet from the level of
bedrock to accommodate a bus terminal below. So, there will be no exca-
vations in his excavation, the appropriate depth having already been
plumbed. And what of the sky above? Will competitors be allowed to
climb the walls of this imposed artistic confinement and reach upward?

In the eighteen-month trajectory of my own thinking about the
site, I began with an idea that the most palpable and urgent record
of the event was the void. Later investigation yielded several architectural interventions that may or may not be to anyone's taste but that
attempted to fill the air with solidity, to restore the urban fabric as

a texture of buildings. Ultimately, though, these seemed inadequate to a memory still very green, just adding more stuff to the long list of concretizations of the ineffable that is the history of memorials and funerary architecture. A few strands, though, remain. That this be a place of gathering and contemplation is central. Below ground, the inescapable and necessary sinews of transportation assert the primacy of unthwarted, encouraged movement as a central answer to terror's dread, its assault on the fundamental right of assembly.

In the end, though, I finally could not discover a convincing necessity for building. Visiting the site over and again I have become more and more convinced of its power and dignity as a space. It is not an extravagant thought. Ground Zero in its voided condition belongs to a family of great spaces in both its scale and proportion. Its edges are already mainly strong and could be strengthened by new building. And, at the end the day, there can be no stronger repository of meaning than the space of its void. Grandeur, dignity, and universal access best mark both tragedy and renewal. Nothing need be built here.

Perhaps the U.S. Government could reduce its contract with Bechtel for rebuilding Iraq by 7 billion and buy the site for America, holding it in memoriam forever.

500ft.

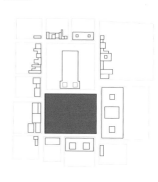

ZOCOLO, MEXICO CITY

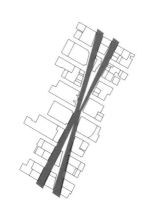

TIMES SQUARE, NY

RED SQUARE, MOSCOW

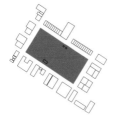

WASHINGTON SQUARE, NY

CENTRAL PARK, NY

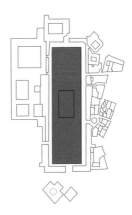

EMAM KHOMEINI SQUARE, ISFAHAN

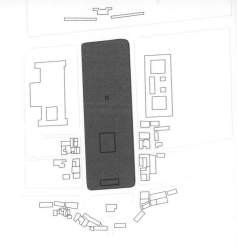

TIENANMIN SQUARE, BEIJING

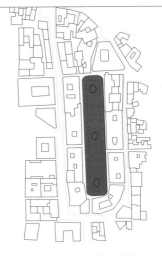

PIAZZA NAVONNA, ROME

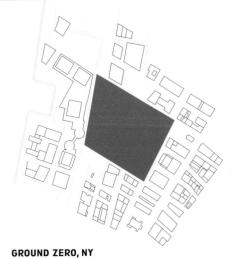

GROUND ZERO, NY

A plan for downtown

THE IMAGES IN THIS BOOK WERE PREPARED
BY THE MICHAEL SORKIN STUDIO

MICHAEL SORKIN
ANDREI VOVK

MITCHELL JOACHIM
JAIR LAITER
MIRAI MORITA
JONATHAN SOLOMON

PHOTOGRAPHY:
PAGE 14: © LAWRENCE A. MARTIN / WWW.GREATBUILDINGS.COM
PAGE 15: OCTOBER 3, 2001 / DEBORAH NATSIOS & JOHN YOUNG ARCHITECTS

BOOK DESIGN: SCOTT DEVENDORF
DISTANT STATION LTD.
WWW.DISTANTSTATION.COM